HOW TO SWAP BATCHES OF COOKIES AND CANDY WITH OTHERS

KATHERINE W. MASHBURN

HOW TO SWAP BATCHES OF COOKIES AND CANDY WITH OTHERS

PLUS, 115 GREAT RECIPES

KATHERINE W. MASHBURN
©2012 By Katherine W. Mashburn
All Rights Reserved

Released October, 2012

No part of this work may be reproduced or transmitted in any form by any means electronic, mechanical, photocopying, recording, or otherwise, without the prior permission from the copyright owner.

Cover Art by CreateSpace.com

For more information, please visit kathymashburnbooks.com

HOW TO SWAP BATCHES OF COOKIES AND CANDY WITH OTHERS

TABLE OF CONTENTS

CHAPTER	PAGE
Acknowledgements and Disclaimer	3
Introduction	4
An Idea in the Baking	6
Directions for Batch-Swapping	13
The Batch-Swap	19
A Rotation of Locations	21
A Schedule of Family Batch-Swaps	22
A Batch-Swap Theme	23
A Surprise Batch-Swap	25
A Neighborhood Batch-Swap	25
A Mystery Batch-Swap	26
A Batch-Swap Cook-Off	26
A Batch Basket for Sharing	27
A Batch-Swap of Cookie Stacks	28
Congratulations, You Are Now Ready To - Plan Your First Batch-Swap	29
Favorite Recipe List for Quick Reference	32
Cookies and Candy Recipes	33
Cakes, Pies, and Other Recipes	85
Conclusion	157
Index	158
References from the Kitchen of…	161

KATHERINE W. MASHBURN

ACKNOWLEDGEMENTS AND DISCLAIMER

I would be remiss not to acknowledge and thank those who have graciously contributed their time and talents to this project. <u>How to Swap Batches of Cookies and Candy with Others</u> would not have been possible without the support and love of those who have encouraged me to stretch my wings; especially Jennifer Mashburn Hambright, Lindsey Kathleen Pruitt, and Rana Elyse Mashburn. I also want to thank Karen M. England and Freida Talley. The feedback and insight they provided was invaluable. Lastly, I must thank everyone who shared recipes for this collection. Their names are listed after the index and beneath each respective recipe.

<u>How to Swap Batches of Cookies and Candy with Others</u> is not intended to be a cookbook; instead it is a collection of recipes from some very fine bakers, including several members of my family, my friends, my neighbors, and my co-workers. The collection of recipes in this book is provided for your personal use and has not in all cases been tested or tried by me personally. Nutritional values for the recipes in this collection are not provided for medical or diet purposes. Different people have different severities to allergies, so please use caution by reading each recipe and its ingredients carefully. Recipes in this collection are not guaranteed to be free of peanuts or other nuts. I do not claim to be a nutritional expert, and therefore do not assume any responsibility or liability of any kind on behalf of the purchaser or user of this book. By choosing to use the recipes in this book, you agree to hold harmless the author and publisher from all claims, suits, proceedings, losses, damages or expenses of any nature. I hope you enjoy this collection of recipes. I welcome your comments or suggestions and invite you to write *How to Swap Batches of Cookies and Candy with Others*, P. O. Box 3962, Dalton, GA 30719.

HOW TO SWAP BATCHES OF
COOKIES AND CANDY WITH OTHERS

INTRODUCTION

First, let me begin by saying this book is not about counting calories, or exercising, or skipping the good stuff used to make delicious cookies, candy, cakes, and pies. In fact, the only exercise you are likely to experience after reading this book is from running back and forth to the kitchen for homemade cookies and candy.

In *How to Swap Batches of Cookies and Candy with Others,* I share several creative ways to organize and host a Cookie Batch Swap with others. In addition, I have assembled a collection of more than 100 great recipes to jumpstart your batch-swapping experience.

Every successful Batch-Swap begins with a great cookie or candy recipe. The recipes included in this book are easy to follow and can be used for any occasion. I hope you will agree after trying one or more of them, that your sweet tooth cravings will be completely satisfied.

I love every recipe in this collection, but I have to say my most favorite is Roberta's Cake (page 147). The late Roberta Fielden Byrd of Jefferson City, Tennessee was not only a great baker; she was also a precious sister-in-law to Elizabeth Fielden.

Every recipe was contributed by special women who, like me, enjoy the art of baking. My personal love of baking and the happiness it brings when I share baked goods with others is the primary reason this book was created. All of the recipes are special for different reasons. I sincerely hope that many of them will become a favorite to you as well. I truly hope you will enjoy *How to Swap Batches of Cookies and Candy with Others*. I am certain you will find it to be a delicious little read!

~Kathy Mashburn~

Happy Swapping!

HOW TO SWAP BATCHES OF COOKIES AND CANDY WITH OTHERS

AN IDEA IN THE BAKING

It was late one night as I sat curled up on my couch channel surfing the television to find a home-shopping network; I promised myself I would not lose sleep again to get a jump on the Christmas season. Due to financial and time restraints, I had begun to dread shopping for Christmas gifts.

This wasn't my first time to do my shopping during the eleventh hour. In fact, it had become almost customary for me to shop during the late hours of the night and into the early morning hours of the next day. I had become addicted to the Home Shopping Network (HSN) and Quick Value Convenience (QVC) channels. I couldn't resist the urge to look for last minute items that were both affordable and unique for every person on my gift list.

I had become addicted to marathon shopping sprees after midnight. The current economic times had made it difficult for many families to afford Christmas shopping and my family was no exception.

So this year, just like most years, I made a concerted effort to find the perfect gifts for my family and friends with the few dollars I had managed to set aside for the occasion.

As I jotted down item numbers for the things I intended to buy, I began to think about how other families with little to no stretched dollars might celebrate the holidays.

Just like most folks, it had become necessary for me to bargain hunt for the least costly gifts for my family, so here

KATHERINE W. MASHBURN

I sat curled up on my sofa with the television remote in hand flipping back and forth between the shopping channels.

On the sheet of notebook paper lying across my lap, I had written the names of my children and grandchildren, my sisters, their spouses, their children, my grandparents, a couple of aunts and uncles, several cousins and friends, and a few neighbors for whom I hoped to buy a gift. Since my list was fairly long, I made a mental note to not spend more than $15 per person. I had to choose my gifts carefully, so I concentrated on the details of each item appearing on the screen to be certain I didn't miss things such as extra shipping costs or automatic renewals.

Being frugal was the only way I could afford to purchase a gift for everyone on my list and for those family members who wished to participate in the ritual we called "Our Annual Exchange".

Each Christmas, it had become tradition for my sisters and me to debate whether we should or should not, or could or could not exchange gifts with each other during the holidays. It was a crazy debate where we rarely agreed on anything, so I had come to dislike the whole process.

At the debate, we would usually gather around the kitchen table sipping coffee or cocoa while eating a slice of pie, or piece of cake, or a handful of cookies. It was here we'd share our thoughts and ideas about gift-giving for the upcoming holiday. Both old ideas and new ideas were bounced around as we collaborated on the best course to take to please everyone. Some of my sisters preferred

HOW TO SWAP BATCHES OF
COOKIES AND CANDY WITH OTHERS

drawing names, while others suggested reducing the spending limit set for each gift. Each year it was customary for the adults in the family to buy a gift for each child who had not yet graduated from high school, but financial hardships had made it difficult for some adults to commit to this custom—especially this year.

So with this in mind, my sisters and I had decided that gifts would not be exchanged this year. Instead, we worked to design a plan that most would agree to like—drawing names. We agreed that anyone who insisted on exchanging gifts had to maintain a maximum cost of $10 per gift. We also agreed that handmade gifts would be preferred over those that cost money, especially if a family did not have money to spend.

Like most families, there is always at least one rebel in the group who adamantly goes against the plan to eliminate gifts, and instead elects to buy gifts for everyone with little or no regard for the suggested spending limits. Although not intentional, these rebels would only make the rest of us feel badly. Even so, we never said anything to them because secretly we appreciated that the kids would each get one more gift in spite of financial hardships.

So it came to pass that our family holidays were celebrated in a manner which embraced both those who could and those who could not.

So let's get back to my midnight Christmas shopping on QVC. Yawning and rubbing my eyes in an attempt to stay awake, I stared at the television watching one item after the other come up for sale. I was restless as I had not seen anything to suit the people I needed to buy for nearly an hour. I stood up to stretch my legs, and then decided I was in need of caffeine if I were going to stay awake long enough to finish my shopping. A clock on the wall ticked methodically, and glancing at it, I realized it was almost three a.m. I was in grave danger of nodding off, so I headed to the kitchen to brew a fresh cup of coffee in my fancy Keurig, one-cup-at-a-time, coffeemaker. I switched the Keurig on and spun the carousel sitting beside it around to select my favorite blend. As the carousel spun, I couldn't help but be tempted by the milk chocolate cocoa flavors nestled in the rack. After a moment, I decided cocoa would be better than my usual coffee. Besides, hot cocoa was almost a guarantee to keep me in a Christmas spirit. I took the K-cup from the carousel, placed it in the maker, and pushed the blue flashing light indicating the machine was ready to brew. In seconds, hot warm cocoa began to fill the Santa mug I had placed beneath the spout and the smell of chocolate filled the air.

I don't know about you, but warm cocoa always puts me in the mood for something sweet to eat, so I turned my attention to the cupboard in search of something to satisfy my sweet craving. After a quick search, I was happy to find a new package of chocolate chip cookies tucked behind a box of cereal. Taking the entire package of chocolate chip cookies and my steaming cup of cocoa with me back to the living room, I settled myself once more on the couch for another round of shopping.

Awe! "Cookies and cocoa", I thought as I shifted my weight to sit more comfortably on the sofa Indian-style.

HOW TO SWAP BATCHES OF COOKIES AND CANDY WITH OTHERS

Almost immediately, I became more alert as I munched the cookies and sipped the cocoa. I continued my search for bargains on the shopping network. The longer I sat on the couch jotting down item numbers and prices, I couldn't help but think how nice it would be if my family could enjoy a simple Christmas with less gifts and more cookies and cocoa. I had heard of cookie exchanges before, but I didn't really know the ins and outs of how to go about organizing or hosting one. It was with this thought in mind that I decided to create my own plan to simplify our Christmas tradition using cookies and cocoa. I enjoyed fellowshipping with my family and friends, and I was certain most of my sisters would be interested in an inexpensive and fun way to fellowship during the holidays.

As the doodles on the paper I held became more of a random list of ideas about organizing and hosting a batch-swap and less about a gift list, I grew more excited about the possibility of swapping batches of cookies with others. As thoughts and ideas filled my head, I quickly scribbled them onto my paper. It was just a few minutes before I had captured a lengthy list of things that would need to be done in order to conduct a fun and successful cookie swap.

I had completely forgotten about Christmas shopping and I had lost all interest in the merchandise parading across the television screen. I was too busy designing a plan for hosting my first anticipated Batch-Swap of cookies to worry about shopping.

The one thing I was pretty clear about was I didn't want to host a cookie party where my guests would come simply to eat the cookies I baked. Instead, I wanted to host an event where my guests would participate in baking and bringing cookies to share similar to a potluck.

Gathering up the half-eaten package of chocolate chip cookies and my empty coffee mug, I headed back to the kitchen.

I admit I had never been an avid baker of cookies, unless you count the frozen Pillsbury varieties from the grocery store. However, I did own several cookbooks that were hidden away in a drawer in my kitchen for longer than I could remember. So at five o'clock in the morning, I pulled a church cookbook from the top of the stack of those I had tucked away. I blew the dust from its cover and went in search of a cookie recipe. I aimlessly flipped through the pages with hopes that one would magically leap from the page, but that didn't happen. After a bit, I closed the book and my eyes, and then reopened it blindly to a random page. It was on page nine that I found a short recipe for Oatmeal Raisin Cookies. The recipe seemed simple enough, so I set about gathering the ingredients to make a batch.

Following the recipe to the letter, I prepared the cookies as directed and placed them in the oven to bake. They smelled delicious, and I was proud of myself. When the cookies were done, I transferred them onto a wire rack to cool and went to wake my children for breakfast. I was sure they'd be excited that I had made homemade cookies for breakfast. I know what you must be thinking – cookies for breakfast? Well, in my defense they were made with

HOW TO SWAP BATCHES OF
COOKIES AND CANDY WITH OTHERS

oatmeal and raisins, which are good-for-you ingredients. As the kids gathered in the kitchen, I proudly announced I had made cookies for breakfast, even though I had secretly practiced making the cookies for a Batch-Swap with my friends. In fact, I had already dog-eared several other pages of cookie recipes with the intention of learning how to make other kinds of cookies to swap with friends.

This is how the idea of Batch-Swapping came about in my kitchen. I decided right then and there that I would host a Batch-Swap within a few weeks, but first I wanted to learn everything I could about baking cookies and candy.

KATHERINE W. MASHBURN

DIRECTIONS FOR BATCH-SWAPPING

Now that you know how this book came about, I can share with you the ins and outs of hosting a successful Batch-Swap. The first thing you should know is that there are no absolute rules or specific protocols to follow when batch-swapping!

Batch-Swapping is simply a way to exchange delicious cookies and candy with your family, friends, neighbors, colleagues, and any other group of individuals you wish to invite to participate with you at a Batch-Swapping event.

My first order of business when planning a Batch-Swap is to determine who the Batch Master will be. This person should serve as the host of the Swap. If you are new to swapping, I recommend that you be the Batch Master until your guests and participants understand the basics of how a Swap should work.

The Batch Master is responsible for planning, organizing, and hosting the Swap. You may want to select more than one Batch Master to facilitate the Swap—especially when a large number of participants are invited to join the Swap. I define a large group as 12 or more participants. Batch-Swaps can be designed for any number of participants regardless of whether the group is large or small.

To begin organizing a Batch-Swap, first identify who will be participating. I call the participants Batch-Bakers. In my experience, I have found batch-swapping to be the most fun with a minimum of 12 Batch-Bakers, but any even number

HOW TO SWAP BATCHES OF
COOKIES AND CANDY WITH OTHERS

of participants will work. Just remember, it takes two to Tango—or to bake cookies for the purpose of swapping.

The next thing you should do is set the date, time, and location of the Batch-Swap. I prefer to rotate locations because it affords families and friends an opportunity to visit in each other's homes in a casual environment. There's nothing like swapping cookies and candy around the kitchen table and fellowshipping with people you love.

After you have determined the basic details, you can decide if you would like to have a theme for your Batch-Swap. For example, you might choose to host a Christmas or Super Bowl-themed swap. It's always fun to make your cookies and candy with a theme in mind. I enjoy making frosted cookies in the shape of stars, bells, and Santa Claus during Christmas swaps; or in the shape of basketballs, footballs, or cheerleading megaphones during a sports-themed event. Be creative! There are countless ways to organize a Swap, and in this book I have shared a few of my favorites.

The Batch Master should prepare and distribute invitations to the invited participants of the Batch-Swap. Generally, I prefer to make my own invitations by designing special flyers or postcards, but it also works well to call your invited participants personally. A phone call is especially important if prospective batch-bakers don't understand how a Batch-Swap works. In this case, they may be reluctant to participate and a phone call can put them at ease and encourage them to join the Swap. Most often, I choose to email my invitations but sometimes I drop them in the regular mail. If it is your first time to host a Batch-Swap, I highly recommend you call your prospective batch bakers and/or participants to build enthusiasm and to briefly explain how the batch swap works.

EXAMPLE OF AN INVITATION

You are invited to participate in a

HOLIDAY BATCH-SWAP

Saturday,
December 5, 2012
2:00 PM
Kathy's Kitchen
123 Baker Street
Cookie Town, USA 12345

The success of this Batch-Swap is dependent on each participant bringing a designated amount of homemade cookies or servings of candy to swap with others. For this HOLIDAY BATCH-SWAP, participants must bring three dozen cookies or individual servings of candy. Participants should also bring an empty platter or tin to use for collecting their assortment of cookies and candy to take home. Coffee, cocoa, and milk will be served.

Kindly RSVP ~ 706-123-4567

HOW TO SWAP BATCHES OF COOKIES AND CANDY WITH OTHERS

You are now ready to set the rules for the Batch-Swap. Rules are necessary to ensure everyone participating in the swap stays on the same page. For example, all cookies or candy brought to the Swap should be homemade. The number of cookies and candy that the Batch Master determines is needed to participate in the swap is determined by the total number of attendees or participants. This is non-negotiable. In other words, if the Batch Master instructs you to bring two dozen cookies, you must bring two dozen cookies. Batch-Bakers should not cheat by bringing less; otherwise, a participant may feel cheated during the swap if they go home with less cookies or candy than everyone one else. At all times it is the Batch Master's job to ensure everyone gets a fair number of cookies or candy during the swap.

Generally speaking, a Batch-Swap is an event to exchange homemade baked goods only, but on rare occasion I have known a few Batch-Bakers to sneak in cookies or candy from a local bakery. I always encourage participants to make their own, but recognizing people have busy lives, I totally understand if someone needs to occasionally bend the rules a bit. However, I don't allow this to become a habit for my batch-bakers. After all, one of the most important reasons to host a Swap is to enjoy homemade cookies and candy we have taken time to bake for each other.

Finally, it's time to plan what you will bake to bring to the Batch-Swap. Depending on the theme, you will decide if you will be swapping your favorite homemade chocolate chip cookies or famous peanut butter treats.

KATHERINE W. MASHBURN

A Batch-Swap is not just a venue where participants sit around the table eating homemade cookies and candy. Whenever I host or serve as the Batch Master, I ask my guests to exchange their recipes with one another.

In this book, you will find more than 100 recipes that I have solicited from my friends, family, neighbors, and co-workers. I hope you will love them as much as I do. I have marked a few of my personal favorites by placing a star at the end of the recipe name.

Let's do the math. It's easy—really! You won't need a degree in mathematics or accounting to determine how many cookies or candy each batch-baker needs to bake to participate in the Swap. For all purposes in this book a batch is defined as one dozen cookies. All you need to do is determine how many dozens or batches of cookies you want each participant to take home with them from the Batch-Swap. You will divide this number by the number of batch-bakers, which will equal how many total cookies each person should bring to swap.

Ok, so I'm sure that was as clear as mud, so let's go through it once more.

I have invited 12 Batch-Bakers to a Batch-Swap and I would like for each of them to take home three dozen assorted cookies at the end of the Swap. Three dozen cookies baked by all 12 participants equals 432 cookies—36 dozen. Of course, things don't always turn out the way you plan, so sometimes it is necessary to improvise.

HOW TO SWAP BATCHES OF COOKIES AND CANDY WITH OTHERS

Let's pretend that I have just learned only 11 of my batch-bakers will be attending the Swap, but I would still like for each participant to leave with three dozen assorted cookies. In order to accomplish this I will ask the 11 batch-bakers attending to makes 40 cookies each or three dozen, plus four additional cookies.

I told you it would easy, but if you are ever in doubt just ask a few batch-bakers to toss in a few extra cookies just to be on the safe side.

Each participant or batch-baker should place their freshly baked cookies or candy on a serving platter. They will place their platter on the serving table when they arrive at the Batch-Swap. Each participant or batch-baker should also bring to each Batch-Swap an empty platter or tin to use to gather their assorted cookies or candy when the Swap begins. It is not mandatory for batch-bakers to provide the recipes for the cookies and candy they bring, but I always encourage my participants to bring a typed copy of their recipe with them to exchange with everyone who is participating.

KATHERINE W. MASHBURN

THE BATCH-SWAP

The day of your Batch-Swap you should decorate your kitchen or dining room according to the theme you have selected to use. If you are not using a particular theme, simply place pretty tablecloths on the table to prepare it for the delicious platters of cookies and candy your batch-bakers are bringing to the Swap.

Arrange the platters of cookies brought to the Swap on the table making an effort to separate like cookies. I place empty bowls or boxes of various sizes under the tablecloth to create a tiered platform on which to place some of the platters to create interest in the design of my cookiescape.

Invite your guests to have coffee, cocoa, hot apple cider, eggnog, sodas, or milk from the drink station you have preset prior to their arrival at the Swap.

Play nice music to set the mood for a great time. Christmas carols add a lovely touch during the holidays; otherwise, I like to choose something akin to elevator music such as classical or instrumentals. Piano or flute music works great as well.

Do not allow your guests to sneak cookies or candy from anyone's platter until all guests have arrived and all baked goods have been placed on the table.

When everyone is ready, ask your guests to rotate around the table picking up a cookie or serving of candy from each platter on display as they move around the table. They will place the cookies and candy they gather in their empty tin

HOW TO SWAP BATCHES OF
COOKIES AND CANDY WITH OTHERS

or on the extra platter they were asked to bring to the Swap. This part of the Batch-Swap is sort of like playing musical chairs, except in a Batch-Swap everyone wins each time they add a cookie or serving of candy to their tin or platter to take home. Participants should continue the rotation until all the cookies and candies are gone. Everyone should end up with three dozen assorted cookies or candies.

KATHERINE W. MASHBURN

A ROTATION OF LOCATIONS

One of the ways my family and I enjoy Batch-Swapping is by rotating the location of where Swaps will be held. Since I have six sisters, this works well. A rotation is not only fun, it allows us an opportunity to visit in each other's homes. We enjoy sipping coffee and eating cookies and candy as we visit and spend valuable time together. Don't get me wrong—sharing delicious cookies and candy with my sisters is always great, but the best benefit to our Batch-Swaps is spending time with one another.

Six works out to be a great number for us since we schedule our Batch-Swaps on a bi-monthly basis. Each year, following our Christmas dinner, we draw months for the coming year. We place slips of paper with February, April, June, August, October, and December written on them in a small basket or jar to be drawn. This is how we do it in my family, but any method of taking turns will work. We set our schedule for Batch-Swaps and leave the planning up to those based on the respective months drawn. Again, this is my family's way of doing things. It's totally up to you to decide how many or how often you or your family would enjoy planning and participating in a Batch-Swap. Be creative and set a plan that works best for you.

HOW TO SWAP BATCHES OF
COOKIES AND CANDY WITH OTHERS

A SCHEDULE OF FAMILY BATCH-SWAPS

Date	Batch Master	Theme
January	Kathy	Confetti Swap
February	None	No Swap
March	Mary Lynn	St. Patty Swap
April	None	No Swap
May	Elizabeth	Spring Fling Swap
June	None	No Swap
July	Melinda	Red, White, and Blue
August	Deborah	Batch Master's Choice
September	Amanda	Sports Swap
October	Karen	Spooky Swap
November	None	No Swap
December	Donna	Jingle Bell Swap

KATHERINE W. MASHBURN

A BATCH-SWAP THEME

This chapter consists of some of my favorite Batch-Swapping themes. Use your imagination to create your own.

Cookie Confetti Batch-Swap: Cookies and candies are decorated with things such as sprinkles in celebration of the New Year.

We Love to Batch-Swap: Cookies and candies are decorated using hearts, or pink, red, and white in celebration of Valentine's Day.

Lucky Batch-Swap: Cookies and candies are decorated in green and white using chocolate coins, leprechauns, and rainbows in celebration of St. Patrick's Day.

Bunny Batch-Swap: Cookies and candies are decorated using chocolate eggs, jelly beans, shredded coconut (grass), peeps or crosses in celebration of Easter.

Spring-Fling Batch-Swap: Cookies and candies are decorated with pretty colors, butterflies, or flowers.

Summer Time Batch-Swap: Cookies and candies are decorated with a picnic team like using red and white frosting in a gingham pattern.

Celebrate Freedom Batch-Swap: Cookies and candies are decorated in red, white, and blue, or use licorice strings to make fireworks in celebration of the 4th of July.

HOW TO SWAP BATCHES OF COOKIES AND CANDY WITH OTHERS

Back-to-School Batch-Swap: Cookies and candies are decorated with a school theme by using tiny pencils, erasers, and apples.

Go Team Batch-Swap: Cookies and candies are decorated or shaped like footballs, basketballs, softballs, baseballs, bowling, and megaphones in celebration of all sports.

Spooky Batch-Swap: Cookies and candies are decorated with ghosts, witches, goblins, and spiders using black, orange, green, and purple in celebration of Halloween.

Batch-Swap to Give Thanks: Cookies and candies are decorated with anything related to the fall season. This one is especially nice since we ask each participant to bring a list of things he or she is thankful for to read aloud to everyone during the swap.

Jingle Bell Batch-Swap: Cookies and candies are decorated with Santa, bells, stars, ornaments, wreaths, and snowmen in celebration of Christmas.

Super Bowl Batch-Swap: Cookies and candies are decorated with footballs, megaphones, or team colors for the teams playing in the Bowl.

KATHERINE W. MASHBURN

A SURPRISE BATCH-SWAP

A surprise swap occurs when batches of cookies and candies are secretly prepared by a group of batch-bakers who are in cahoots to surprise an unsuspecting friend or family member. In other words, you and your other batch-bakers show up at a person's home or work place with batches in hand to swap. Of course, you will need to adjust your cookie totals to make up for the lucky recipient whom you are surprising. Basically, the surprising batch-bakers will make extra cookies on behalf of the person being surprised.

For example, six batch-bakers are making cookies for the surprise swap, but seven people will be attending counting the person you are surprising. The six batch-bakers will make enough cookies for all seven participants to take home 2 dozen each.

A NEIGHBORHOOD BATCH-SWAP

A neighborhood batch-swap occurs when two or more households make plans to gather for the primary purpose of swapping cookies and candies. I say primary purpose because a batch-swap also presents a perfect opportunity to plan a neighborhood yard sale or block party to coincide with the batch-swap. Once it is decided which neighbor is to host the swap, take extra care to notify everyone else in the neighborhood of the details. After all, no one appreciates being left out, especially when there are cookies and candies involved.

HOW TO SWAP BATCHES OF
COOKIES AND CANDY WITH OTHERS

A MYSTERY BATCH-SWAP

A mystery batch-swap occurs when participants randomly draw a small strip of paper with a specific kind of cookie or candy written on it from a jar. Participants draw from the jar the name of the specific cookie or candy they are to make and then should do research to learn how to make the cookies or candies. The Batch Master or host should follow up to be certain each participant has what he or she needs to participate in the swap such as date, time, location, and deadlines.

A BATCH-SWAP COOK-OFF

A batch-swapping cook-off occurs when groups of friends or family come together for the purpose of baking cookies onsite in a cook-off. Two batch-bakers are randomly selected to compete in a cookie cook-off using the same recipe and ingredients for a specific cookie selected by the group. When it is my turn to be the Batch Master, I sometimes allow the batch-bakers the freedom to tweak the recipe to their liking for interest and variety. While the batch-bakers are busy whipping up fresh batches of cookies, the rest of the group sits around sipping coffee, cocoa, or other beverages as they fellowship and wait for delicious cookies to be pulled from the oven. The winner of the batch-swapping cook-off wins the honor of selecting a new Batch Master for the next batch-swap.

KATHERINE W. MASHBURN

A BATCH BASKET FOR SHARING

Another fun thing I like to do is organize batch baskets for sharing. To do this, I solicit the help of batch-bakers who graciously agree to make their cookies and candies to be shared with others. It's easy to share batches. We just make our batches as though we were going to participate in a neighborhood batch-swap, but instead of swapping the cookies and candies they make, the group divvies them up into batches and places them into small baskets or decorative tins to be distributed to a local nursing home, a group of teachers, firefighters, policemen, or other service providers.

NOTE: If you choose to share cookies with residents of a nursing home, be sure to take along a few baskets of sugar-free cookies or candies in case you meet someone who must limit their sugar intake due to health reasons. It is also important to ask all recipients of your cookies if they have any allergies to nuts.

One of my favorite ways to share cookies and candies is by divvying up a batch into small stacks. When doing this, I place two or three cookies or candies into small cellophane bags and tie them with a pretty ribbon. These small bags of cookies and candies make a perfect gift to share with small children in daycare or Sunday school group.

There are unlimited ways to share cookies. It's another opportunity to be creative in the kinds of cookies and packaging you select to be shared.

HOW TO SWAP BATCHES OF COOKIES AND CANDY WITH OTHERS

A BATCH-SWAP OF COOKIE STACKS

I love to make batch-swapping stacks! A batch-swapping stack is made by placing cookies in a clean and empty Pringles can. Batch-bakers prepare their cookies as usual; but instead of bringing them to a Batch-Swap on platters to be distributed to participants, they are brought to the swap pre-packaged in clean and decorated Pringles canisters to be swapped. My preference is to place my stack of cookies into slender cellophane bags tied with a pretty ribbon before sliding them down into the Pringles can. This will keep your cookies fresh for a longer period of time.

KATHERINE W. MASHBURN

CONGRATULATIONS, YOU ARE NOW READY TO PLAN YOUR FIRST BATCH-SWAP!

By now your head is probably spinning with countless ideas for ways to organize your own personal Batch-Swaps. I hope you find it both fun and easy to swap batches of cookies and candy with others after reading this book. Cookie Batch-Swaps are easy to organize and easy to host for any group of people including daycares, school classrooms, churches, or office personnel. Batch-Swapping is the perfect way to fellowship with your friends and family; especially during the holidays. Some of the following suggestions may have been mentioned previously in the book, but I find them worth repeating to ensure a successful Batch-Swap.

Setting the Date – When planning a Batch-Swap, you should try to set a date that will work best for the majority of your intended guests or participants. For example, if most of your participants work during the week, you may want to choose a Saturday or Sunday afternoon to ensure good attendance. I enjoy scheduling batch-swaps around the holidays, so the first weekend in December works great when kicking off the Christmas season with my family and friends.

Preparing the Invitations – It's easy to prepare invitations for a Batch-Swap because you can manage them in a variety of ways. Being an avid crafter, I generally prefer to make my invites using scrapbook paper, ribbons, and markers, or sometimes I design a snazzy postcard on the

HOW TO SWAP BATCHES OF
COOKIES AND CANDY WITH OTHERS

computer. Others may choose to purchase a simple party invitation from a local store and fill in the blanks. Regardless of how you prepare invitations, you will want to be certain to include details about the event including the number of dozen cookies that are needed to participate, when and where, etc. This is particularly true since most people may not have participated in a cookie-swap before. Don't forget to remind your guests to bring an empty tin or platter to gather their cookies on during the swap. Send online invitations to your family and friends, or mail them via regular mail. Be creative and have fun designing a theme that suits your ideas for the batch-swap.

Preparing for the Batch-Swap – On the day of the swap, prepare a space large enough to accommodate your guests and participants. One of my favorite parts of hosting a batch-swap is to prepare a Cookiescape for my guests to place their platters of cookies and candy on when they arrive. I create my Cookiescape by setting tables with tiered spaces on which to set platters of cookies and candy. This is easily done by placing upside down bowls or boxes of varied sizes under a bunched tablecloth. This will create a tiered look for the display of cookies and candy, plus it makes it easier to pick up a cookie from staggered levels when the guests begin to participate in the rotation of swapping cookies and candy. Be certain your table or cookiescape has sufficient room to allow guests and participants to move around freely.

In addition to preparing a cookiescape, you will want to set up a drink station where you might offer coffee, cocoa, hot apple cider, eggnog, sodas, or milk. For ease and variety, I sometimes set up a Keurig coffeemaker with several coffee and tea flavors from which my guests may choose. Since most guests will take home their assorted collection of cookies and candy from the swap, I also like to set up a few other varieties of snacks near the drink station for my guests to enjoy. Chips and dips (or something salty) are a great contrast to the sweet cookies and candy.

Guests and participants will most likely enjoy listening to music while they swap cookies and candy; this is especially nice during the holidays. Most guests will enjoy singing along to Christmas carols during your holiday swap.

Providing Party Favors or Door Prizes – Although it is not necessary to offer favors or door prizes at your batch-swap, it can be fun and easy to do. For favors, I enjoy sharing the recipe for the cookies or candy I bring to the swap by printing them on heavy cardstock and cutting them into 4x6 cards to handout to each participant. Sometimes, I tie them to small wooden spoons with ribbon. Instead of favors, you may enjoy providing a few door prizes to give away via a random drawing. Some of my favorite door prizes are measuring cups, cookie mixes, pot holders, or bottles of vanilla or other flavorings.

HOW TO SWAP BATCHES OF
COOKIES AND CANDY WITH OTHERS

ON THIS PAGE, LIST YOUR FAVORITE RECIPES IN THIS COLLECTION FOR A QUICK REFERENCE ANYTIME

Don't forget to write down the name of the recipe and its page number.

1. ROBERTA'S CAKE - Page 147

KATHERINE W. MASHBURN

COOKIES AND CANDY RECIPES

The collection of recipes in this book is from the kitchens of many of my family, my friends, my neighbors, and my co-workers. I hope you enjoy making them in your kitchen, just as I have.

Peanuts

A FAVORITE CANDY
From the Kitchen of Elizabeth Fielden

Ingredients
1 lb. white chocolate or candy coating
½ cup peanut butter
1 ½ cups miniature marshmallows
1 ½ cups roasted, unsalted peanuts
1 ½ cups Rice Krispies

Directions
Melt chocolate in a 200° F oven (or in microwave according to directions on the package). Stir in peanut butter, and then add in other remaining ingredients. Drop by rounded teaspoons onto wax paper. Cool before serving. Recipe yields approximately 6 ½ dozen. Enjoy.

HOW TO SWAP BATCHES OF
COOKIES AND CANDY WITH OTHERS

BAKER'S ONE BOWL CHOCOLATE BLISS COOKIES

From the Kitchen of Barbara Callahan

Ingredients

2 packages (8 squares each) Baker's semi-sweet baking chocolate, divided
¾ cup firmly packed brown sugar
½ stick butter, softened
2 eggs
1 teaspoon vanilla
½ cup self-rising flour
2 cups chopped Planters cocktail peanuts (optional)

Directions

Preheat oven to 350° F. Coarsely chop 8 of the chocolate squares; set aside. Microwave the remaining 8 squares in a large microwaveable bowl on high for 2 minutes; stirring after 1 minute until chocolate is completely melted. Add sugar, butter, eggs, and vanilla; stir until well blended. Add in flour; mix well. Stir in chopped chocolate and nuts. Drop dough by rounded tablespoons 2 inches apart on ungreased baking sheets. Bake 12 to 13 minutes or until cookies are puffed and shiny. Cool cookies on baking sheet for 1 minute before transferring to wire racks. Cool completely before serving. Recipe yields approximately 2 ½ dozens. NOTE: Substituting walnuts or pecans for peanuts is optional. Enjoy.

KATHERINE W. MASHBURN

BLACK BEAN BROWNIES (Gluten Free)
From the Kitchen of Lisa Dickey

Ingredients
1 (15 oz.) can black beans, rinsed and drained
3 eggs
3 tablespoons vegetable oil
1/3 cup cocoa powder
1 pinch salt
1 teaspoon vanilla extract
¾ cup sugar
1 teaspoon coffee (optional)
1 cup chocolate chips, divided (optional)
½ cup coarsely chopped walnuts (optional)

Directions
Preheat oven to 350° F. Lightly grease an 8 inch square baking pan; set aside. Combine the black beans, eggs, oil, cocoa powder, salt, vanilla extract, sugar, and instant coffee in a blender or food processor until smooth. Stir in ½ cup of chocolate chips and walnuts (if using). Pour the mixture evenly into the prepared pan. Sprinkle the remaining ½ cup chocolate chips (if using) on the top of the mixture. Bake 25 to 30 minutes or until the top is dry and the edges start to pull away from the sides of the pan. Cool completely on a wire rack, and then cut brownies into a desired size and shape. NOTE: I like to tweak the recipe by adding a little cinnamon or a little cayenne pepper, or sometimes both. It gives the brownies a little kick. I do not use the coffee, but I do use the chocolate chips. I also substitute part Stevia for part of the sugar. Experiment and have fun. Enjoy.

HOW TO SWAP BATCHES OF
COOKIES AND CANDY WITH OTHERS

BLONDE BROWNIES

From the Kitchen of Kathy Mashburn

Ingredients
1 ½ cups self-rising flour
1 ¼ cups packed dark brown sugar
1 ¼ cups mini M&M's
¾ cup (1 ½ sticks) butter, melted and cooled
2 teaspoons vanilla extract
2 eggs

Directions
Prepare a 9 inch baking pan by lightly greasing or spraying with non-stick cooking spray. Combine butter, sugar, eggs, and vanilla in a large bowl, and then slowly add the flour and blend well. Fold in the mini M&M candies. Spread batter evenly into baking pan. Bake brownies at 350° F for approximately 25 minutes or until a toothpick interested into the center comes out clean. Cool completely before cutting into squares. NOTE: Serve with a scoop of vanilla ice cream and a drizzle of chocolate syrup, if desired. Enjoy.

KATHERINE W. MASHBURN

Brown Sugar

BUCKEYES
From the Kitchen of Rachel Owens

Ingredients
1 – 1 lb. box of powdered sugar
1 cup peanut butter
2/3 cup butter
1 – 8 oz. Hershey candy bar
¼ bar paraffin wax

Directions
Combine powdered sugar, butter, and peanut butter; mix well. Roll into 1 inch size balls. Melt paraffin wax and chocolate together on low heat, or in a microwaveable safe bowl. Dip balls into melted chocolate to coat; place on wax paper to set. Store the Buckeyes in the refrigerator in an airtight container. Enjoy.

Chocolate

CARAMEL APPLEJACK BALLS
From the Kitchen of Donna Stone Brown

Ingredients
1 stick margarine
1 – 14 oz. package caramels
1 teaspoon vanilla
3 cups Applejack cereal

Directions
Melt margarine and caramels in a large saucepan; covered while melting over low heat. Remove from heat after completely melted. Add vanilla and Applejack cereal; stir well to coat all cereal. Butter the palms of yours hands and roll the coated cereal into 2 inch balls. Place on wax paper to set. Enjoy.

KATHERINE W. MASHBURN

CARAMEL BROWNIES WITH NUTS
From the Kitchen of Shauna Leatherwood

Ingredients
1 – 12 oz. package semi-sweet chocolate chip morsels, divided
1 box Brownie mix (prepared as directed on package)
¾ cups firmly packed brown sugar
1 cup pecan pieces, divided
1 bag of chocolate covered caramels (Rolos candy/about 40 pieces), chopped and divided
Vanilla ice cream (optional)

Directions
Preheat oven to 375° F; lightly grease a baking sheet. In large mixing bowl, combine all ingredients to make the brownies and add ¼ cup brown sugar. Fold in 1 ½ cups chocolate chip morsels. Pour batter into baking pan and smooth evenly. In a plastic baggy combine half of the nuts and the remaining brown sugar; shake to coat. Sprinkle nuts over top of the batter. Bake for approximately 20 minutes or until a toothpick inserted in the center comes out clean.

Remove from oven, and then scatter ½ of the caramels over top of hot brownie; lightly press caramels into the cake. Cut the remaining caramels into small pieces and scatter over top with the remaining nuts.

Melt the remaining chocolate morsels in a microwaveable bowl on HIGH for 1 minute. If needed, add increments of

HOW TO SWAP BATCHES OF
COOKIES AND CANDY WITH OTHERS

10 seconds cooking time until chocolate melts completely. Drizzle melted chocolate over brownie. Cut into squares and serve warm with a scoop of ice cream, if desired. Brownies are also delicious served cool. Enjoy.

Walnuts and Chocolate Morsels

KATHERINE W. MASHBURN

Brownies

CARAMEL CORN
From the Kitchen of Cindy McEntyre

Ingredients
1 bag of microwaveable popcorn (popped)
1 stick butter
½ cup light brown sugar
8 large marshmallows

Directions
Pour popped popcorn in to a large bowl (removing all un-popped kernels). In small saucepan, melt butter and brown sugar. Continue to cook for approximately 2 minutes on stovetop until sugar dissolves completely. Remove from heat and add marshmallows; stirring again until completely melted. Pour over popped corn; stir or toss to coat.

Pour coated popcorn out onto a cookie sheet. Place in 300° F to 325° F preheated oven to crisp for 10 to 12 minutes. Stir halfway through baking time. WATCH CAREFULLY TO PREVENT BURNING. Cool 3 to 4 minutes before transferring to a bowl; cool completely. Enjoy.

HOW TO SWAP BATCHES OF
COOKIES AND CANDY WITH OTHERS

Caramel

CARAMEL PECAN COOKIES

From the Kitchen of Karen England

Ingredients
½ tube refrigerated sugar cookie dough
1 package caramels
1 tablespoon heavy whipping cream
1 package pecan halves
1 cup chocolate chips

Directions
Cook cookie dough into ¼ inch slices. Place two inches apart on ungreased cookie sheet. Bake at 350° F for 8 to 10 minutes or until lightly brown. Allow to cool.

Melt caramels and cream together; stir until smooth. Spoon melted caramel on center of each cookie, and then top with a pecan halve in middle of caramel.

Melt chocolate chips; stir until smooth. Spoon the melted chocolate over the caramel. Allow cookies to set before serving. Recipe yields approximately 1 ½ dozens. Enjoy.

KATHERINE W. MASHBURN

Whipping Cream

CHESS BARS
From the Kitchen of Cindy McEntyre

Ingredients and Directions for First Layer
1 box Butter Pecan cake mix
1 stick of butter (melted)
1 egg
½ cup chopped pecans

Mix together melted butter and egg; stir into dry cake mix. Add pecans, and then press into a 13x9 baking pan you have sprayed with non-stick cooking spray.

Ingredients and Directions for Second Layer
1 stick of butter (melted)
1 – 8 oz. package cream cheese (softened)
2 eggs
1 box (1 lb.) powdered sugar
1 cup chopped pecans
1 teaspoon vanilla extract

Beat melted butter, softened cream cheese, and eggs with a mixer; fold in powdered sugar and blend well. Add vanilla extract, and then the pecans. Spread this on top of First

HOW TO SWAP BATCHES OF COOKIES AND CANDY WITH OTHERS

Layer in pan. Bake at 325° F for 45 to 55 minutes. Cool completely before cutting into squares. Enjoy.

Bake

Stir

Whip

KATHERINE W. MASHBURN

CHOCOLATE CHIP COOKIES
From the Kitchen of Kathy Mashburn

Ingredients
3 cups semi-sweet chocolate chips
4 to 5 cups self-rising flour
2 tablespoons vanilla extract
3 eggs
1/2 cup of milk
3 ¾ cups brown sugar
2 ½ cups shortening

Directions
Preheat oven to 350° F. In a large bowl, cream shortening and brown sugar. Add eggs, milk, and vanilla: stir until well blended. Slowly add in the flour; mix well. Gently fold in chocolate chips. Drop batter by tablespoonful about 2 inches apart on ungreased baking sheet. Bake 8 to 12 minutes or until they are golden brown. Cool completely on wire racks. Recipe yields 5 dozen. Enjoy.

Chocolate Chips

HOW TO SWAP BATCHES OF
COOKIES AND CANDY WITH OTHERS

Condensed Milk

CHOCOLATE COOKIE CANDY
From the Kitchen of Elizabeth Fielden

Ingredients
1 (14 oz.) can Eagle Brand sweetened condensed milk
2 squares Baker's chocolate
1 (3 ½ oz.) can flaked coconut
1 teaspoon vanilla
2 cups chopped pecans
1 tablespoon margarine

Directions
In a double boiler cook milk chocolate and coconut until stiff. When it becomes stiff enough to hold its shape; remove from heat and add vanilla, pecans, and margarine. Form candy into small balls; place on a butter-greased baking sheet. In moderate oven, bake at 325° F for about 8 minutes; be careful not to overcook. Once done; remove from baking sheet as quickly as possible. These cookies are excellent for gift giving. Enjoy.

KATHERINE W. MASHBURN

CHOCOLATE SURPRISE COOKIES
From the Kitchen of Barbara Callahan

Ingredients
1 ½ sticks of butter (softened)
1/3 cup firmly packed light brown sugar
1 ½ teaspoon vanilla
1 ½ cups of all-purpose flour
1/8 teaspoon cinnamon
25 Hershey kisses
1 ½ tablespoons confectioner sugar
¾ teaspoon unsweetened cocoa

Directions
Preheat oven to 350° F. Combine butter and brown sugar in a medium bowl; beat with an electric mixer on medium speed until light and fluffy. Add vanilla. Combine flour and cinnamon in another medium bowl; slowly add flour mixture to batter mixture; mix well. Shape dough into 1 inch balls. Flatten balls into a 2 inch round shape. Place the rounds 1 inch apart on a 2 ungreased baking sheets. Place a chocolate kiss in center of each round, and then enclose kiss in the dough. Bake for 15 minutes or until golden brown. Combine confectioner sugar and cocoa in a small bowl; sprinkle it over hot cookies. Allow cookies to cool on baking sheets for 10 minutes before transferring to wire racks to cool completely. Recipe yields 2 dozen. Enjoy.

HOW TO SWAP BATCHES OF
COOKIES AND CANDY WITH OTHERS

CHRISTMAS WREATH COOKIES
From the Kitchen of Cyndi Best Owenby

Ingredients
½ to 1 whole box of Rice Krispies cereal
1 bag marshmallows
1 bag of candy Red Hots
Green food coloring

Directions
Melt marshmallows and Rice Krispies together on stovetop. Add 3 or 4 drops of food coloring; stir until mixed well. Remove from stove after mixing; shape into Christmas wreaths using your fingers; place on wax paper. Form wreaths with or without the center hole. Place red hot candies around wreaths; trim with licorice ribbons for detail. Allow to cool before serving. Enjoy.

KATHERINE W. MASHBURN

CORNFLAKE COOKIES
From the Kitchen of Elizabeth Fielden

Ingredients
1 cup light corn syrup
1 cup creamy peanut butter
1 teaspoon vanilla extract
6 to 7 cups of cornflake cereal

Directions
Combine ingredients (except cereal) in a heavy saucepan. Cook over low heat; stir. Add cereal; stir well. Drop by tablespoon onto wax paper. Allow cookies to set. Recipe yields approximately 4 dozen. Enjoy.

HOW TO SWAP BATCHES OF
COOKIES AND CANDY WITH OTHERS

CORNFLAKE FLOWERS
From the Kitchen of Barbara Callahan

Ingredients
4 cups cornflakes (crushed to 1 ½ cups of fine crumbs)
1 can (3 ½ oz.) flaked coconut
½ cup seedless raisins
1 (15 oz.) can Eagle Brand sweetened condensed milk
1 teaspoon vanilla

Directions
In a bowl, combine cereal crumbs, coconut, and raisins. Add condensed milk; mix well. Spoon leveled tablespoons of mixture onto a well greased baking sheet. Bake in moderate oven at 350° F for 10 minutes or until lightly brown. Recipe yields approximately 3 ½ dozen. Enjoy.

KATHERINE W. MASHBURN

Almonds

COW PIES
From the Kitchen of Elizabeth Fielden

Ingredients
2 cups or 2 oz. milk chocolate chips
1 tablespoon shortening
½ cup raisins
½ cup chopped slivered almonds

Directions
In a double boiler over simmering water, melt chocolate chips and shortening; stir until smooth and remove from heat. Add raisins and almonds, and then drop by tablespoons onto wax paper. Chill before serving. Recipe yields approximately 2 dozen. Enjoy.

HOW TO SWAP BATCHES OF
COOKIES AND CANDY WITH OTHERS

CROCKPOT CANDY
From the Kitchen of Elizabeth Fielden

Ingredients
2 lbs. white chocolate
1 – 4 oz. bar German sweet chocolate
1 – 18 oz. package semi-sweet chocolate chips
1 – 24 oz. jar roasted peanuts (unsalted)

Directions
Put white chocolate, German chocolate and semi-sweet chocolate in a Crockpot on low heat. Cook for 2 hours; do not stir. When cooking time ends, add peanuts; stir gently. Drop by teaspoon onto wax paper to cool. Recipe yields approximately 100 pieces. Enjoy.

White Chocolate

KATHERINE W. MASHBURN

EASY PECAN STICKY BUNS
From the Kitchen of Kathy Mashburn

Ingredients
½ cup firmly packed brown sugar
3 tablespoons butter, melted and divided
1 tablespoon light corn syrup
¾ cup chopped pecans, divided
1 package refrigerated crescent rolls
1 teaspoon cinnamon

Directions
Preheat oven to 375° F. Spray an 8 inch square baking dish with non-stick cooking spray. In a small bowl, combine ¼ cup brown sugar, 2 tablespoons butter, and corn syrup; mix well until smooth. Spread over bottom of baking dish.

Unroll crescent roll dough; press seams together to form a large rectangle. Brush with remaining melted butter. Sprinkle with remaining brown sugar, cinnamon, and remaining pecans. Beginning at the wide end; roll up dough (jelly-roll style); chill roll for 5 minutes. Using a sharp knife, cut roll into 9 equal slices. Place each slice cut-side down in baking dish. Bake 18 to 20 minutes or until golden brown. Remove from oven and immediately invert onto a serving platter; being careful with the hot melted sugar. Cool slightly before serving. Spread with glaze, if desired. For glaze, mix together ½ cup powdered sugar, ½ teaspoon vanilla, and 2 tablespoons milk. Enjoy.

HOW TO SWAP BATCHES OF
COOKIES AND CANDY WITH OTHERS

FORGOTTEN COOKIES

From the Kitchen of Sherry Moss

Ingredients
2 egg whites
2/3 cup sugar
¼ teaspoon salt
1 cup pecans
1 cup chocolate chips

Directions
Preheat oven to 350° F. Beat egg whites until foamy. Add sugar; beat until stiff. Add salt; mix well. Fold in pecans and chocolate chips. Drop by teaspoon onto a cookie sheet lined with aluminum foil. Place cookies in oven, and then switch it to off. Leave cookies in closed oven overnight. Enjoy.

Pinch of Salt

KATHERINE W. MASHBURN

FRENCH BUTTER COOKIES
From the Kitchen of Karen England

Ingredients
½ cup butter
½ cup vegetable shortening
1 ½ cups sifted powdered sugar
1 teaspoon vanilla
2 cups flour
¼ teaspoon salt
1 teaspoon cream of tarter
1 egg

Directions
Cream butter and shortening together until light and fluffy, and then add powdered sugar; beat until smooth. Add egg and vanilla; beat well. Gradually stir in sifted dry ingredients; mix well. Chill before shaping into small balls and placing on an ungreased cookie sheet. Slightly flatten balls with a fork. Bake at 350° F for about 10 to 12 minutes. Do not overcook. Enjoy.

Butter

HOW TO SWAP BATCHES OF
COOKIES AND CANDY WITH OTHERS

Baking Soda

GRANNY MOORE'S CHRISTMAS COOKIES
From the Kitchen of Yvette Dunn

Ingredients
½ cup butter
1 cup brown sugar
1 egg, beaten
1 large jar of mixed candied fruits
1/3 cup sour cream (or pet milk)
1 ¾ cups of flour
½ teaspoon baking soda
1 cup chopped dates
1 cup chopped nuts

Directions
Mix together ingredients and store in refrigerator overnight. Drop by teaspoonfuls onto baking sheets. Bake at 350° F for about 12 minutes or until golden brown. Enjoy.

KATHERINE W. MASHBURN

HEALTHIER NO BAKE COOKIES
From the Kitchen of Lisa Dickey

Ingredients
1 ripe banana, mashed well
1 cup sugar
¼ cup of cocoa powder
½ cup non-fat milk
½ cup peanut butter
A pinch of salt
1 teaspoon pure vanilla extract
3 cups instant oatmeal

Directions
Place all ingredients, except vanilla and oats, in a medium sauce pan and bring to a boil over medium heat; stir often. Boil mixture to boil for 1 minute; remove from heat. Cool mixture for 1 minute before adding vanilla and oats; stir until well combined. Drop by teaspoonfuls onto wax paper; cool completely. Enjoy.

Oatmeal

HOW TO SWAP BATCHES OF
COOKIES AND CANDY WITH OTHERS

HOMEMADE PEANUT BUTTER CUPS
From the Kitchen of Yvonne Burns

Ingredients
1 – 11 ½ oz. Package (milk) chocolate chips, divided
3 tablespoons vegetable shortening, divided
1 ½ cups confectioner sugar
1 cup creamy peanut butter
¼ cup (or ½ stick) butter, softened

Directions
Begin by lining a 12 cup muffin tin with paper baking cups. In a small saucepan, melt 1 1/3 cups chocolate chips and 2 tablespoons of shortening over low heat; stir just until mixture is smooth. Allow to cool slightly. Mixture should be pourable. Starting halfway up each paper cup, spoon about 2 tablespoons of mixture over the inside of cups; completely covering bottom of each cup. Place muffin tin in refrigerator for 30 minutes to chill chocolate cups until firm.

In a large mixing bowl, combine confectioner sugar, peanut butter, and butter; mix well. NOTE: Mixture will be dry. Spoon evenly into cooled chocolate cups and press down firmly.

Place remaining chocolate chips and shortening in a small saucepan and melt over low heat; stir just until mixture is smooth. Spoon equal amounts into chocolate cups; spread chocolate mixture over top of peanut butter mixture to cover completely. Cover peanut butter cups with plastic wrap and chill for 2 hours or until firm. Enjoy.

Mix
Blend
Fold

HOW TO SWAP BATCHES OF
COOKIES AND CANDY WITH OTHERS

LACE COOKIES
From the Kitchen of Cindy McEntyre

Ingredients
1 cup uncooked oatmeal (not the instant oatmeal)
1 cup sugar
¼ teaspoon baking powder
1 egg, slightly beaten
2 tablespoons, plus 1 teaspoon flour
½ teaspoon salt
¼ lb. melted butter or margarine
2 teaspoons vanilla extract

Directions
Combine dry ingredients, and then add melted butter, beaten egg, and vanilla. Line a cookie sheet with parchment paper or aluminum foil. Drop ½ teaspoon of batter on paper: leave room for batter to spread. Bake at 350° F for 6 to 8 minutes. The cookies should start to brown on the edge and almost to the center. (You may have to experiment with the first pan.)

Allow cookies to cool completely before removing from paper or peeling from aluminum foil. NOTE: Do not be tempted to use more than ½ teaspoon of batter for each cookie. They must be small enough to brown from the edges to at least halfway into the cookie without burning. If cookies are too big, the edges will burn before the cookie can cook long enough to be done in the center. Enjoy.

KATHERINE W. MASHBURN

Graham Crackers

MAGIC COOKIE BARS
From the Kitchen of Elizabeth Fielden

Ingredients
1 stick butter
1 ½ cups graham cracker crumbs
1 – 14 oz. can Eagle Brand condensed milk
6 – 8 oz. chocolate chips
2 cups flaked coconut, divided
¾ cups chopped nuts

Directions
Melt butter in baking pan; sprinkle graham cracker crumbs over butter. Pour condensed milk over graham cracker crumbs. Sprinkle chocolate chips on top, and then add 1 ¾ cups of flaked coconut. Scatter nuts on top and bake at 350° F for 25 minutes or until coconut turns golden brown. Enjoy.

HOW TO SWAP BATCHES OF
COOKIES AND CANDY WITH OTHERS

MARTHA WASHINGTON CANDY
From the Kitchen of Darlene Lucas

Ingredients and Directions for Candy Centers
1 ½ cups of chopped pecans
1 stick of margarine, melted
1 ½ boxes powdered sugar
Dash of salt
1 can of Eagle Brand condensed milk
1 teaspoon vanilla
2 small cans of coconut

Mix together all ingredients and form into balls. Chill 4 hours.

Ingredients and Directions for Candy Coating
¼ block paraffin wax
12 oz. chocolate chips

Melt wax on stovetop over medium heat. Add chocolate chips; stir until melted and evenly mixed. Dip balls in chocolate and place on wax paper to cool. Enjoy.

KATHERINE W. MASHBURN

MIXED NUTS MILLIONAIRES CANDY
From the Kitchen of Elizabeth Fielden

Ingredients
1 cup light corn syrup
½ cup granulated sugar
½ cup firmly packed light brown sugar
½ cup butter
1 cup heavy whipping cream
1 teaspoon vanilla extract
1 cup chopped pecans
1 cup chopped walnuts
1 cup chopped almonds
½ cup chopped cashews
1 – 16 oz. package chocolate flavored candy coating

Directions
Begin by lining baking sheets with parchment or waxed paper. In a medium saucepan, combine corn syrup, granulated sugar, and brown sugar; cook over medium heat. Stir frequently until candy thermometer registers 250° F. Add butter; stir until completed melted. Add heavy cream and cook until candy thermometer registers 242° F. Remove from heat; stir in vanilla, pecans, walnuts, almonds, and cashews. Drop nut mixture by teaspoonfuls onto prepared baking sheets. Cool for 30 minutes. Use a fork to dip each candy in melted chocolate candy coating. Recipe yields approximately 10 dozen. Enjoy.

HOW TO SWAP BATCHES OF
COOKIES AND CANDY WITH OTHERS

NO COOK PEANUT FUDGE
From the Kitchen of Brenda Blaylock

Ingredients
1/3 cup margarine or butter
½ cup corn syrup
¾ cup peanut butter
½ teaspoon salt
1 teaspoon vanilla extract
½ cup confectioner sugar
4 cups chopped peanuts

Directions
In a mixing bowl, combine margarine or butter with corn syrup, salt, and vanilla; blend well. Stir in sugar last; blend again until smooth. Press fudge out on pan or plate. Sprinkle chopped nuts on top and press slightly into fudge. Cut into squares to serve. Recipe yields approximately 2 pounds. Enjoy.

Peanuts

KATHERINE W. MASHBURN

Vanilla

OATMEAL RAISIN COOKIES
From the Kitchen of Barbara Callahan

Ingredients
1 ½ cups self-rising flour
1 cup firmly packed brown sugar
1 ½ sticks of butter (softened)
1 teaspoon vanilla
1 ½ cups quick cooking oats
1 cup seedless raisins

Directions
Preheat oven to 350° F. Grease 3 baking sheets. Place the brown sugar and butter in a large mixing bowl; beat with an electric mixer on high until light and fluffy. Beat in eggs and vanilla until smooth. Gradually stir in the flour using a wooden spoon until thoroughly combined. Blend in oats and raisins. Drop the dough by rounded spoonfuls 1 ½ inches apart on prepared baking sheets. Flatten the dough slightly with a fork. Bake for 12 minutes or until golden brown. Cool on baking sheets for 2 minutes before transferring to wire racks. Serve warm or at room temperature. Recipe yields approximately 3 dozen. Enjoy.

HOW TO SWAP BATCHES OF
COOKIES AND CANDY WITH OTHERS

OLD FASHIONED POTATO CANDY

From the Kitchen of Linda Allen

Ingredients
½ cup (preferably homemade) mashed potatoes
5 cups powdered sugar
1 teaspoon vanilla extract
¼ teaspoon salt
4 tablespoons peanut butter (approximately)

Directions
Put mashed potatoes, vanilla, and salt in a bowl; add 1 cup of powdered sugar at a time while kneading with your hands until mixture becomes a firm fudge-like consistency. You may need a bit more or less of the powder sugar depending on how the mashed potatoes were made. Make adjustments depending on the texture of the mix. It should be firm and dry enough to keep its shape, but not too dry that would cause it to crumble.

Divide the mixture in half; sprinkle work surface and rolling pin with powdered sugar and roll the potato candy into a 1/3 inch thickness. Spread a thin, but not too thin, layer of peanut butter on top (about a ¼ inch). If you use too much peanut butter it squishes out the sides when you are rolling the candy up.

Gently roll into a loaf and cover with plastic wrap or wax paper. Chill 1 to 2 hours before cutting the loaf into ½ inch thick slices. Each loaf yields approximately 12 slices. Enjoy.

KATHERINE W. MASHBURN

Pecans

ORANGE NO-BAKE COOKIES
From the Kitchen of Elizabeth Fielden

Ingredients
¾ lb. powdered sugar
1 – 1 lb. package vanilla wafers, crumbled very fine
1 stick butter or margarine, melted
1 cup chopped nuts (pecans or walnuts)
1 – 6 oz. can of frozen orange juice
1 – 7 oz. bag of flaked coconut

Directions
Mix all ingredients, except coconut, together. Shape dough into small balls and roll in them in coconut. Recipe yields approximately 4 dozen. Enjoy.

HOW TO SWAP BATCHES OF
COOKIES AND CANDY WITH OTHERS

OREO TRUFFLES

From the Kitchen of Jennifer Mashburn Hambright

Ingredients
1 – 8 oz. package cream cheese (softened)
1 – 15.5 oz. package Oreo cookies (finely crushed to make approximately 4 ½ cups)
2 packages (8 squares each) Baker's semi-sweet chocolate (melted)

Directions
Combine cream cheese and 3 cups of the crushed cookies; mix well. Shape into 1 inch balls (about 45); dip into the melted chocolate. Place on baking sheet covered with wax paper. Sprinkle with remaining cookie crumbs; refrigerate until firm. Store the truffles in a sealed container in the refrigerator. NOTE: Using any flavor of cookie works great. I prefer dipping regular flavored Oreos in melted white chocolate. Mint or Berry Oreos are great in melted milk chocolate. Enjoy.

KATHERINE W. MASHBURN

PEANUT BUTTER COOKIES
From the Kitchen of Lisa Dickey

Ingredients
1 cup peanut butter
1 cup sugar
1 egg

Directions
Combine ingredients; mix well. Roll into 1 inch balls and flatten in the traditional crisscross pattern with a fork. Bake at 350° F for 10 to 12 minutes. Enjoy.

PEANUT BUTTER COOKIES
From the Kitchen of Natalie Smith

Ingredients
1 cup peanut butter smooth
1 cup sugar
1 egg
½ teaspoon vanilla

Directions
Mix all ingredients together. Chill before rolling into small balls (marble). Bake at 325° F for 8 to10 minutes or until lightly brown. Enjoy.

HOW TO SWAP BATCHES OF
COOKIES AND CANDY WITH OTHERS

PEANUT BUTTER CRÈME COOKIE CUPS
From the Kitchen of Linda Allen

Ingredients
½ cup pecan pieces
1 package Big Deluxe refrigerated chocolate chip cookies
½ cup white chocolate chips
¼ cup peanut butter

Directions
Preheat oven to 350° F. Place paper or foil baking cups in each of 12 regular-sized muffin cups (cupcake pan). Lightly coat each cookie with pecans; press nuts into dough. Place each cookie (flat side down) in muffin cups. Bake 18 to 22 minutes or until edges are golden brown. Cool in muffin tin on cooling rack for approximately 30 minutes. The centers of the cookies will sink slightly, but make a deeper well in each one by using the bottom of a rounded measuring spoon. In a small microwaveable bowl, melt white chocolate chips on medium power for 1 to 1 ½ minutes; stir halfway through cooking time and continue cooking until smooth. Stir peanut butter into the melted chocolate; blend until smooth. Spoon approximately 2 teaspoons of peanut butter mixture into each cookie cup. Remove the cups from the muffin tin and store covered in an airtight container. NOTE: Sometimes I melt about 14 oz. of chocolate chips and a sweetened condensed milk in the microwave for 90 seconds and spoon this mixture into the cookies. Enjoy.

KATHERINE W. MASHBURN

PEANUT BUTTER SURPRISES
From the Kitchen of Barbara Early

Ingredients
1 cup butter, softened
1 cup crunchy peanut butter
¾ cup firmly packed brown sugar
¾ cup granulated sugar
2 eggs
1 ½ teaspoon vanilla
2 ½ cups all-purpose flour
1 teaspoon baking powder
1 teaspoon baking soda
½ teaspoon salt
2 cups coarsely chopped miniature Reeses cups

Directions
Preheat oven to 350° F. Cream the butter, peanut butter, sugars, eggs, and vanilla together until fluffy. Stir flour, baking powder, baking soda, and salt together; gradually stir in dry ingredients into creamed mixture. Add chopped peanut butter cups. Drop by heaping teaspoons onto ungreased baking sheets. Bake 12 to 15 minutes or until lightly browned. Remove from baking sheets; cool on wire racks. Recipe yields approximately 5 dozen. Enjoy.

HOW TO SWAP BATCHES OF COOKIES AND CANDY WITH OTHERS

Peppermint

PEPPERMINT BARK
From the Kitchen of Elizabeth Fielden

Ingredients
1 – 24 oz. package white chocolate candy coating
10 peppermint sticks, crushed
3 drops peppermint flavoring
2 drops red food coloring

Directions
Place a large piece of wax paper on countertop or table. Place candy coating in top of a double boiler over boiling water. Reduce heat to low and cook until candy coating is completely melted; stirring occasionally. Remove from heat; stir in crushed peppermint, peppermint flavoring, and food coloring. Spread candy onto wax paper. After candy cools, cut into squares or break into pieces. Enjoy.

KATHERINE W. MASHBURN

PUMPKIN FUDGE
From the Kitchen of Sabrina Owens

Ingredients
3 cups granulated sugar
¾ cup butter, melted
2/3 cup evaporated milk
½ cup canned pure pumpkin
2 tablespoons corn syrup
1 teaspoon pumpkin pie spice
1 – 12 oz. package white chocolate morsels
1 – 7 oz. jar marshmallow crème
1 cup pecans, chopped and toasted (optional, but highly recommended)
1 teaspoon vanilla extract

Directions
Line a 9 inch square pan with aluminum foil; spray with non-stick cooking spray. Stir together the sugar, butter, milk, pumpkin, corn syrup, and spice in a 3 quart saucepan over medium heat. Cook and stir constantly until a candy thermometer registers 234° F (soft ball stage) or for about 12 minutes. Remove from heat and quickly stir in the remaining ingredients; blend well. Pour fudge into prepared pan. Let stand for 2 hours or until the fudge is completely cooled. Cut into desired size squares. Recipe yields about 3 pounds. Enjoy.

HOW TO SWAP BATCHES OF
COOKIES AND CANDY WITH OTHERS

REINDEER COOKIES
From the Kitchen of Karen England

Ingredients
1 – 17 ½ oz. package of peanut butter cookie mix
1/3 cup canola oil
1 egg
1 package miniature pretzels
1 package semi-sweet chocolate chips
Red hot candies

Directions
Combine cookie mix, oil, and egg; blend well. Shape into a 7 ½ inch roll and wrap in plastic wrap. Refrigerate for 1 hour before cutting into 1/4 inch slices. Place slices two inches apart on ungreased cookie sheet. Make an indention 1/3 of the way down the sides of each slice. Add pretzels for antlers, chocolate chips for eyes, and a red hot candy for the nose. Bake at 350° F for 9 to 11 minutes or until light brown. Allow to cool. Recipe yields approximately 2 ½ dozen. Enjoy.

Pretzels

KATHERINE W. MASHBURN

ROBERTA WHOOPIE PIES
From the Kitchen of Barbara Early

Ingredients and Directions for Filling
Make filling first and chill until needed.
8 oz. cream cheese, softened
16 oz. container cool whip, thawed
1 cup powdered sugar
½ cup granulated sugar
1 King size Hershey candy bar, grated

Mix all ingredients together; chill for 2 hours

Ingredients and Directions for Cookies
2 boxes Swiss Chocolate cake mix
2/3 cup butter, melted
2 eggs
¼ cup water

Combine cake mix, butter, eggs, and water; mix well. Drop by tablespoons onto cookie sheets lined with parchment paper. Bake at 375° F for 8 to 10 minutes. Cool cookies on wire racks. Once the cookies cool, assemble Roberta Whoopie Pies by sandwiching a tablespoon of filling between two of them. Enjoy.

HOW TO SWAP BATCHES OF
COOKIES AND CANDY WITH OTHERS

ROCKY ROAD SQUARES
From the Kitchen of Karen England

Ingredients
4 – 4 ½ oz. milk chocolate bars
3 cups miniature marshmallows
¾ cup chopped walnuts

Directions
Partially melt chocolate over hot water. Remove melted chocolate from heat; beat until smooth. Stir marshmallows and nuts into the chocolate. Spread in buttered 8x8x2 baking pan; chill until firm. Cut into squares to serve. Enjoy.

RUM BALLS
From the Kitchen of Karen England

Ingredients
2 cups vanilla wafer cookies, finely chopped
2 tablespoons cocoa
¼ cup rum or brandy
1 cup chopped pecans
1 cup powdered sugar
2 tablespoons white corn syrup

Directions
Combine all ingredients; mix well. Shape into 1 to 1 ½ inch balls. Roll balls in powdered sugar or cocoa. Store tightly covered for at least one week before serving. Enjoy.

KATHERINE W. MASHBURN

SCALY BARK
From the Kitchen of Cindy McEntyre

Ingredients
Graham crackers
1 stick butter
1 stick margarine
½ cup sugar
½ to 1 cup chopped pecans

Directions
Line a baking sheet with aluminum foil; spray foil with non-stick cooking spray. Line the baking sheet with a layer of whole graham crackers. Sprinkle chopped nuts over the crackers.

Cook butter, margarine, and sugar in a saucepan. Let the mixture come to a boil and continue to boil for 1 minute; pour mixture over the crackers and nuts. Place in a 350° F oven and bake for 10 minutes. Remove to cool, and then break into pieces. NOTE: Placing the bark in the refrigerator for about an hour will allow it to harden well. Enjoy.

HOW TO SWAP BATCHES OF
COOKIES AND CANDY WITH OTHERS

SCOTCH BARS

From the Kitchen of Rachel Morehead

NOTE: Scotch bars are kissing cousins to Brownies with a butter scotch flavor and a top well peppered with chocolate chips.

Ingredients
1 cup sifted flour
½ teaspoon baking powder
1/8 teaspoon baking soda
½ teaspoon salt
½ cup chopped nuts
1/3 cup shortening
1 cup firmly packed brown sugar
1 tablespoon hot water
1 egg, slightly beaten
1 teaspoon vanilla
½ cup Baker's semi-sweet chocolate chips

Directions
Sift flour, baking powder, soda, and salt together. Add nuts; mix well. Melt shortening in saucepan; remove from heat. Add brown sugar and water; mix well. Allow to cool slightly. Add egg and vanilla; blend well. Add flour mixture, a small amount at a time; mix well after each addition. Pour batter into greased 9x9x2 inch pan. Sprinkle chocolate chips on top. Bake at 350° F for 20 to 25 minutes or until toothpick inserted in center comes out clean. (DO NOT OVERBAKE.) Allow to cool in pan before cutting into desired size bars. Enjoy.

KATHERINE W. MASHBURN

SCRUMPTIOUS RICE KRISPIES
From the Kitchen of Barbara Callahan

Ingredients
1 can of Eagle Brand condensed milk
1 large package marshmallows
1 box Rice Krispies
1 – 16 oz. package Kraft caramels
¼ cup butter

Directions
Melt in double boiler the condensed milk, caramels, and butter. Dip marshmallows in caramel mixture; roll in Rice Krispies. NOTE: You may melt caramel, butter, and milk in the microwave by using a microwaveable safe bowl. Start with 3 minutes; stir and add increments of 1 minute cooking time until mixture is well blended. Enjoy.

HOW TO SWAP BATCHES OF
COOKIES AND CANDY WITH OTHERS

S'MORES TREATS
From the Kitchen of Lisa Dickey

Ingredients
9 cups Honey Graham cereal (like Golden Grahams)
¾ cup light corn syrup
3 tablespoons butter
11 ½ oz. package milk chocolate chips
1 teaspoon vanilla
3 cups mini-marshmallows

Directions
Grease a cookie sheet with butter. Measure 9 cups of graham cereal into a large mixing bowl. In medium saucepan over medium heat, combine corn syrup, butter, and milk chocolate chips. Stir constantly until the chocolate chips are melted and ingredients are combined well. Remove from heat and stir in vanilla. Pour over cereal and stir quickly until cereal is coated with the melted chocolate. Add in marshmallows. Pour mixture onto cookie sheet and using a slightly damp hand press into the pan. Enjoy.

Marshmallows

KATHERINE W. MASHBURN

Self-rising Flour

SNICKERDOODLES
From the Kitchen of Barbara Callahan

Ingredients
½ cup butter
½ cup shortening
2 ¼ cups self-rising flour
1 ½ cups sugar
2 eggs
3 tablespoons sugar
1 teaspoon cinnamon

Directions
Cream together butter and shortening, and then add sugar and eggs; mix thoroughly. Add flour; mix until smooth. Roll cookies into 1 inch balls and coat with sugar and cinnamon mixture (made by mixing sugar and cinnamon) before baking. Bake at 400° F for 6 to 8 minutes. Enjoy.

HOW TO SWAP BATCHES OF
COOKIES AND CANDY WITH OTHERS

STRAWBERRIES

From the Kitchen of Elizabeth Fielden

Ingredients

2 cups chopped pecans
2 – 6 oz. boxes strawberry Jell-o
1 – 14 oz. can Eagle Brand condensed milk
1 – 7 oz. can coconut, flaked
1 cup red colored sugar
1 package slivered almonds
Green food coloring

Directions

Mix pecans, strawberry Jell-o, condensed milk, and coconut together. Put in refrigerator for 1 hour only. Shape into strawberries and roll in red sugar. Dye almonds green and stick one in the top of each strawberry to garnish. Recipe yields approximately 4 dozen medium-size strawberries. Place strawberries in airtight container and store in refrigerator. Enjoy.

KATHERINE W. MASHBURN

Butterscotch

UNBAKED CARAMEL COOKIES
From the Kitchen of Barbara Callahan

Ingredients
2 cups sugar
¾ cups butter
1 – 6 oz. can of Pet evaporated milk
1 – 4 oz. box instant butterscotch pudding mix
3 ½ cups quick cooking oatmeal

Directions
Combine sugar, butter, and evaporated milk in a saucepan and bring to a rolling boil. Remove from heat. Add pudding and oatmeal; mix thoroughly. Cool 15 minutes before dropping rounded tablespoons onto wax paper. Recipe yields approximately 5 dozen. NOTE: You may vary recipe with any flavor of instant pudding. Enjoy.

HOW TO SWAP BATCHES OF
COOKIES AND CANDY WITH OTHERS

WHITE CHOCOLATE PEANUT BUTTER COOKIES

From the Kitchen of Elizabeth Fielden

Ingredients
1 box Ritz crackers
1 pound white chocolate
1 regular size jar creamy peanut butter

Directions
Cover countertop with wax paper. Spread peanut butter between crackers until all crackers are used. Melt white chocolate in double boiler. Dip peanut butter crackers in the melted chocolate until completely covered. Place on wax paper to cool. Place cookies in an airtight container to store. Enjoy.

KATHERINE W. MASHBURN

CAKES, PIES, AND OTHER RECIPES

Although the focus of this book is on cookies and candy, I could not pass up the opportunity to share some really great recipes for cakes and pies too. I hope you enjoy making them as much as I do.

AUNT GWEN'S POUND CAKE
From the Kitchen of Gwen Brown Pritchett and Natalie Smith

Ingredients
1 cup shortening
1 stick butter
3 cups sugar
5 eggs
3 cups plain flour
1 cup sweet milk
½ teaspoon baking powder
1 teaspoon vanilla

Directions
Mix shortening, sugar, and butter. Add eggs one at a time; mix well. Mix dry ingredients and add alternately with milk; add vanilla. Bake for 1 hour and 25 minutes at 325° F. NOTE: You may vary recipe by adding 4 tablespoons of cocoa for chocolate pound cake or a can of flaked coconut for a coconut pound cake. Enjoy.

HOW TO SWAP BATCHES OF
COOKIES AND CANDY WITH OTHERS

BAPTIST POUND CAKE
From the Kitchen of Elizabeth Fielden

Ingredients
3 cups sugar
1 stick butter
½ cup Crisco
5 eggs
3 cups all-purpose flour
½ teaspoon baking powder
Pinch of salt
1 cup sweet milk
1 tablespoon butter & nut flavoring

Directions
DO NOT PREHEAT OVEN. Beat together shortening, butter, and sugar. Add eggs one at a time: beat well after each egg. Sift flour, salt, and baking powder together and add alternately with milk to the mixture. Add flavorings. Grease and flour Bundt pan, or a 10 inch tube pan, or a large loaf pan. Pour batter in pan of your choice. IMPORTANT: PLACE IN A COLD OVEN. Turn oven to 350° F and bake for about 1 hour and 15 minutes or until toothpick inserted in the center comes out clean. Allow to cool 3 to 5 minutes before removing from pan. NOTE: You may substitute Crisco with an additional ½ cup butter or margarine, if desired. Cake will stay fresh longer. Enjoy.

KATHERINE W. MASHBURN

BANANA SPLIT CAKE
From the Kitchen of Cyndi Best Owenby

Ingredients and Directions for Crust
2 cups graham cracker crumbs
½ cup butter or margarine, melted

Mix together graham cracker crumbs and butter. Press into the bottom of an ungreased 9x13 inch cake pan and refrigerate 10 to 12 minutes.

Ingredients and Directions for Filling
2 to 4 small boxes instant vanilla pudding mix

Prepare instant pudding as directed on package; spread over chilled crust. Use as much or as little pudding as you desire.

Ingredients and Directions for Toppings
4 large bananas
1 – 20 oz. can of pineapple, crushed and drained
1 – 12 oz. container frozen whipped topping, thawed
1 bottle Fudge ice cream topping
½ cup chopped walnuts or pecans
¼ cup of quartered maraschino cherries

Slice bananas on top of filling; spread crushed pineapple on top of bananas. Spread whipped topping on top of the pineapple. In the microwave, warm fudge topping slightly and drizzle on top of the whipped topping. Garnish top with nuts and cherries. Refrigerate at least 4 hours before

HOW TO SWAP BATCHES OF COOKIES AND CANDY WITH OTHERS

serving, but I prefer to refrigerate overnight. This Banana Split Cake is very rich and yields approximately 15 servings. Enjoy.

Beat

Chop

Mix

KATHERINE W. MASHBURN

BASKIN ROBBINS PIE
From the Kitchen of Elizabeth Fielden

Ingredients and Directions for Layers

Layer 1 – 1 cup of self-rising flour, 1 stick butter, and ½ cup chopped pecans mixed well. Pat into pie pans and bake 20 minutes at 350° F.

Layer 2 – 8 oz. cream cheese (softened), 1 cup confectioner sugar, ½ of 16 oz. container of cool whip mixed together; spread over cooled crusts.

Layer 3 – 1 box of chocolate (or any flavor) instant pudding mix prepared as directed on package; pour over Layer 2.

Layer 4 – Top with remaining cool whip, whole pecans, and shavings from a Hershey candy bar. Refrigerate pie until ready to serve. Enjoy.

HOW TO SWAP BATCHES OF
COOKIES AND CANDY WITH OTHERS

BUTTERMILK PIE
From the Kitchen of Rachel Owens

Ingredients
1 ½ cups sugar
1 cup buttermilk
½ cup Biscuit mix
1/3 cup butter, melted
1 teaspoon vanilla extract
3 eggs

Directions
Preheat oven to 350° F and grease 9 inch pie pan. Combine all ingredients in a large mixing bowl; beat on medium speed for 1 minute with electric mixer. Pour pie mixture into greased pan; bake for approximately 50 minutes or until toothpick inserted in the center comes out clean. Allow to cool for 5 minutes before serving. Enjoy.

KATHERINE W. MASHBURN

CHERRY STREUSEL CHEESECAKE
From the Kitchen of Missy Gibson Hightower

Ingredients
1 pouch (1 lb, 1.5 oz.) Betty Crocker oatmeal cookie mix
½ cup firm butter
2 – 8 oz. packages cream cheese, softened
½ cup sugar
2 tablespoons all-purpose flour
1 teaspoon vanilla
1 egg
1 can of Cherry pie filling
¼ cup chopped walnuts

Directions
Preheat oven to 350° F. Grease bottom and sides of 9x13 inch baking pan. Place cookie mix in a bowl and cut in butter until mixture is crumbly and coarse. Reserve 1 ½ cups crumb mixture for later. Press remaining crumbs in bottom of the pan; bake for 10 minutes.

Meanwhile, in a large bowl beat together cream cheese, sugar, flour, vanilla, and egg until smooth. Spread this mixture evenly over partially baked crust. Spoon pie filling evenly over cream cheese mixture; sprinkle reserved crumbs over the top. Scatter chopped walnuts on the top of the crumbs. Bake cheesecake for 35 to 40 minutes or until it is golden brown. Cool 30 minutes before refrigerating; chill for 2 hours. Enjoy.

Cream Cheese

CHESS CAKE

From the Kitchen of Christy Crump

Ingredients for Layer 1
1 – 18.25 oz. package yellow cake mix
2 eggs
½ cup butter, melted

Ingredients for Layer 2
1 – 8 oz. package cream cheese, softened
½ cup butter, melted
2 eggs
4 cups confectioners' sugar

Directions
Preheat oven to 325° F (165 degrees C); grease and flour a 9 x13 inch baking pan. Layer 1: In a large bowl, mix together cake mix, eggs, and melted butter from Layer 1 ingredients; blend well. Pour this batter into prepared pan.

Layer 2: In another bowl, beat cream cheese until smooth. Blend in melted butter, eggs; gradually beat in the confectioners' sugar. Pour this batter over the crust mixture already in the pan. Bake for 1 hour. Allow to cool before serving. Enjoy.

KATHERINE W. MASHBURN

CHOCOLATE CHIP POUND CAKE
From the Kitchen of Brooke Keeler

Ingredients
1 box Duncan Hines yellow cake mix
1 small box of instant chocolate pudding mix
4 eggs
½ cup vegetable oil
½ cup warm water
1 – 8 oz. package cream cheese
1 teaspoon vanilla
8 oz. of chocolate chips

Directions
Thoroughly mix all ingredients (add in chocolate chips last). Bake in a tube pan at 350° F for 1 hour or until a toothpick inserted in the center comes out clean. Enjoy.

Pudding Mix

HOW TO SWAP BATCHES OF
COOKIES AND CANDY WITH OTHERS

CHOCOLATE DELIGHT

From the Kitchen of Brooke Keeler

Ingredients

1 cup plain flour
½ cup butter (room temperature)
1 cup chopped pecans
1 cup confectioner sugar
1 – 16 oz. container cool whip
1 – 8 oz. package cream cheese
1 small package instant vanilla pudding mix
1 small package instant chocolate pudding mix

Directions

Mix together flour, butter, and pecans. Press into a 9x13 inch baking pan. Bake at 350° F for 20 to 25 minutes. Allow to cool completely. Mix 1 cup cool whip, sugar, and cream cheese; spread over cooled crust.

Mix both pudding mixes with milk until smooth. Spread pudding mixture over cream cheese layer and top with the remaining cool whip. Chill overnight before serving. Keep refrigerated. Enjoy.

KATHERINE W. MASHBURN

CHOCOLATE PIE
From the Kitchen of Brooke Keeler

Ingredients
1 cup sugar
6 rounded tablespoons flour
2 tablespoons cocoa (not rounded, use more for richer pie)
3 cups sweet milk
4 egg yolks (save whites for meringue)
4 tablespoons butter
2 teaspoons vanilla
2 baked pie shells

Directions
Mix all ingredients together; cook over medium heat stirring constantly until thickened. Pour into pie shells and top with meringue, if desired.

Ingredients and Directions for Meringue
4 egg whites
½ cup sugar
1 teaspoon vanilla

Beat egg whites until stiff; add sugar a little at a time. Add vanilla last. Spread onto pies and brown under a broiler for a few seconds. Recipe yields 2 pies. Enjoy.

HOW TO SWAP BATCHES OF
COOKIES AND CANDY WITH OTHERS

CHOCOLATE PECAN COCONUT PIE

From the Kitchen of Brenda Blaylock

Ingredients
1 cup chocolate chips
4 eggs
1 can coconut, flaked
2 sticks butter
1 cup sugar
1 cup pecans

Directions
Melt butter and chocolate chips together; add sugar, eggs, coconut, and pecans. Pour mixture into pie shell and bake at 350° F for 40 minutes. Cool completely before cutting. Recipe yields 1 deep dish or 2 regular crust pies. Enjoy.

KATHERINE W. MASHBURN

CINNAMON BUN PIE
From the Kitchen of Kathy Mashburn

Ingredients
1 ¾ sticks butter (melted and divided)
1 cup chopped pecans
½ cup sugar
1 tablespoon cinnamon
1 package refrigerated flaky canned biscuits (8 biscuits)

Directions
Preheat oven to 375° F. Coat bottom of a deep dish pie plate with 2 tablespoons of melted butter; set aside. In a small mixing bowl, combine pecans, sugar, and cinnamon; mix well. Sprinkle ¼ of the pecan mixture over bottom of pie plate.

Separate each biscuit into 3 layers. Reserve ¾ cup of melted butter before dipping each biscuit layer into the remaining melted butter being careful to coat each side completely. Layer 8 biscuit pieces in bottom of the pie plate covering the previous pecan mixture. Repeat pecan mixture and biscuit layers too more times. Top off the pie with remaining pecan mixture. Drizzle pie with the reserved melted butter and bake 20 to 25 minutes or until biscuits are golden and cooked through. Allow pie to cool for 10 minutes before inverting onto a serving platter. Slice into wedges and serve warm. Enjoy.

HOW TO SWAP BATCHES OF
COOKIES AND CANDY WITH OTHERS

CITRUS PUCKER-UP CAKE

From the Kitchen of Linda Allen

Ingredients
1 box of lemon cake mix
½ cup mayonnaise
½ teaspoon lemon extract
1 cup buttermilk
Lime curd (recipe included)
Orange whipped cream cheese frosting (recipe included)

Directions
Preheat oven to 350° F. Spray 2 – 9 inch cake pans with non-stick cooking spray; set aside. In a large bowl, combine cake mix, mayonnaise, lemon extract, and buttermilk; mix well for 2 to 3 minutes. Divide the batter evenly into prepared cake pans and bake for 20 to 25 minutes or until toothpicks inserted in the center comes out clean.

Remove cakes from oven and allow cooling for 10 minutes in the pans before removing them; cool completely. On a serving plate with a raised edge, place the first layer and cover with lime curd. Do not worry if the curd runs out when you place the second layer on top. Spread or pipe the cream cheese frosting on the sides and top of the cake to finish. Cover the cake and place in the refrigerator to chill for at least 1 hour. Enjoy.

Ingredients and Directions for Lime Curd
1 cup sugar

¾ cup lime juice
1 tablespoon lime zest
4 tablespoons butter (room temperature)
2 eggs, beaten

Combine sugar, juice, zest, and butter in the top of a double boiler over simmering water. Stir until sugar has dissolved and butter has melted. Continue to cook for at least 5 minutes; stirring constantly. Use ½ cup of the hot mixture to temper the eggs. Slowly add egg mixture back into the pot and continue cooking until mixture thickens; stirring constantly. Allow curd to cool in the refrigerator for at least 1 hour before applying to cake.

Ingredients and Directions for Orange Whipped Cream Cheese Frosting
4 oz. cream cheese, softened
½ stick butter, softened
2/3 cup sugar (or sweetener of your choice)
The juice and zest from 1 medium orange
½ container of whipped topping

In a medium bowl, cream together cream cheese and butter until smooth. Add sugar, juice, and zest; blend well. Fold in whipped topping. Cover the Citrus cake (or any other cake) with frosting. Enjoy.

HOW TO SWAP BATCHES OF
COOKIES AND CANDY WITH OTHERS

CREAM CHEESE POUND CAKE
From the Kitchen of Sherry Moss

Ingredients
3 sticks butter (not whipped)
3 cups sugar (or 3 cups confectioner sugar)
Dash of salt
1 – 8 oz. package cream cheese
6 large eggs
1 ½ teaspoons vanilla
3 cups sifted flour or 2 ½ cups cake flour and ½ cup self-rising flour

Directions
Cream together butter, sugar, salt, and cream cheese; beat in 1 egg at a time. Add vanilla and flour slowly; mix well. Pour batter into a tube pan sprayed with non-stick cooking spray and bake for 1 ½ hours or until toothpick inserted in the center comes out clean. Enjoy.

KATHERINE W. MASHBURN

CREAMY BANANA PUDDING
From the Kitchen of Elizabeth Fielden

Ingredients
1 – 14 oz. can Eagle Brand condensed milk
1 ½ cups of cold water
1 small package instant vanilla pudding mix
1 – 8 oz. container cool whip
Vanilla wafer cookies
Bananas

Directions
Whisk condensed milk and water in a large bowl; add instant pudding mix. Whisk for 2 minutes more to blend well. Chill 5 minutes before folding in the cool whip.

Assemble by spooning pudding mixture into the bottom of a 2 ½ quart glass serving bowl. Layer wafers, bananas, and pudding mixture in the bowl. Repeat layers ending with pudding mixture on top. Chill and garnish as desired. Enjoy.

Bananas

Sprinkle

CRUSTLESS COCONUT PIE
From the Kitchen of Barbara Callahan

Ingredients
2 cups milk
¾ cup sugar
½ cup flour
4 eggs
½ stick butter
1 teaspoon vanilla
1 1/3 cups coconut, flaked

Directions
Place all ingredients in a blender and blend on low speed for 3 minutes. Pour into a greased 9 inch pie plate. Sprinkle with coconut. Bake at 350° F for 40 minutes. Recipe yields 1 – 9 inch pie. Enjoy.

KATHERINE W. MASHBURN

CRUSTLESS PUMPKIN PIE
From the Kitchen of Elizabeth Fielden

Ingredients
4 eggs, beaten
1 – 15 oz. can pumpkin
1 – 12 oz. can of evaporated milk
1 ½ cups sugar
2 teaspoons pumpkin pie spice
1 teaspoon salt
1 box yellow cake mix
1 cup chopped pecans or walnuts
1 cup butter, melted
1 – 8 oz. container cool whip, extra chopped nuts, and cinnamon for garnish (optional)

Directions
Combine eggs, pumpkin, evaporated milk, sugar, spice, and salt; mix well. Pour into an ungreased 9x13 inch baking pan. Sprinkle dry cake mix and nuts over top. Drizzle with melted butter; do not stir. Bake at 350° F for 45 minutes to 1 hour. Test for doneness using a toothpick. Serve with cool whip and sprinkle with nuts and cinnamon, if desired. Recipe yields 8 to 10 servings. Enjoy.

HOW TO SWAP BATCHES OF
COOKIES AND CANDY WITH OTHERS

Apples

DRIED APPLE CAKE
From the Kitchen of Brooke Keeler

Ingredients
3 eggs
2 cups sugar
1 cup butter
3 tablespoons buttermilk
1 teaspoon baking soda
1 teaspoon vanilla
3 cups plain flour
A pinch of salt
9 inch cake pans
Apples cooked in sugar

Directions
Combine all ingredients; mix well. Use enough batter to cover bottom of cake pans. Bake at 350° F until light brown. Make 6 layers total and stack with cooked apples between each layer and on top. Cut apples into chunks, sprinkle with sugar, and cook over medium heat until soft; stir occasionally. Enjoy.

KATHERINE W. MASHBURN

EASY ICE CREAM CAKE
From the Kitchen of Kathy Mashburn

Ingredients
16 mini vanilla or strawberry ice cream sandwiches
2 jars fudge topping
1 ½ cups of chopped pecans (or your favorite nuts)
1 – 16 oz. container cool whip
1 package of Oreo cookies, crushed
Marciano cherries for garnish

Directions
Layer ice cream sandwiches in 9x13 inch glass baking dish. Cover sandwiches with layers of fudge topping, crushed Oreos, cool whip, and nuts ending with cool whip on top; freeze until solid. Garnish with cherries, if desired. Enjoy.

Pies

HOW TO SWAP BATCHES OF
COOKIES AND CANDY WITH OTHERS

EASY WHITE CHOCOLATE CHEESECAKE
From the Kitchen of Barbara Callahan

Ingredients
1 – 8 oz. package cream cheese, softened
2 – 4 oz. boxes of instant white chocolate pudding mix
2 cups cold milk
1 – 8 oz. container cool whip
2 graham cracker crusts

Directions
Mix cream cheese and ½ cup of milk with a mixer until smooth. Add in instant pudding mix and remaining milk; mix well. Fold cool whip into mixture. Spoon into crusts and refrigerate. NOTE: Different kinds of crusts like chocolate graham cracker or Oreo work well with this recipe. Enjoy.

KATHERINE W. MASHBURN

FAT-FREE BANANA SPLIT CAKE
From the Kitchen of Lisa Vickery

Ingredients and Directions for Crust
2 ½ cups graham cracker crumbs
1 stick butter or margarine, melted
1 tablespoon sugar

Mix ingredients together; pat into pan and place in refrigerator until crust is set.

Ingredients and Directions for Filling
2 – 8 oz. packages cream cheese (softened at room temperature)
½ cup powdered sugar
1 small box instant white chocolate pudding mix (or French vanilla)
½ cup milk
1 teaspoon vanilla extract
1 – 8 oz. and 1 – 16 oz. container cool whip
4 -5 bananas, sliced
1 – Large can of crushed pineapple, drained well
1 – Carton of fresh strawberries, sliced
1 – Package strawberry glaze
1 cup pecans
1 – Small jar cherries

Beat cream cheese until completely smooth. In separate bowl, whisk together instant pudding mix and milk until smooth. Fold pudding mixture into cream cheese followed by small container cool whip. Spread over chilled graham

HOW TO SWAP BATCHES OF COOKIES AND CANDY WITH OTHERS

cracker crust. Top with sliced bananas, crushed pineapple, sliced strawberries (mixed with strawberry glaze), cool whip, pecans, and cherries. Refrigerate to set. Enjoy.

Add

Combine

Stir

KATHERINE W. MASHBURN

FLAN
From the Kitchen of Cindy McEntyre

Ingredients
1 – 12 oz. can of evaporated milk
1 can of Eagle Brand condensed milk
5 eggs (3 whole eggs, 2 egg yolks)
½ cup granulated sugar
½ teaspoon vanilla
¼ teaspoon salt

Directions for Caramel
Make first by using 1 cup of granulated sugar. In a 2 quart stainless steel bowl add the cup of sugar. Over medium heat, cook the sugar and do not leave it unattended. You will see the sugar turn into a liquid state. Using pot holders take the bowl and start to shake the sugar back and forth in the bowl. In about 5 minutes, it should all be turning to liquid and will be a caramel color. As soon as the sugar is completely dissolved and it has turned the color of caramel candy, use pot holders to roll the bowl causing the caramel to cover the inside of the bowl. You must work quickly. Set the bowl aside and allow the caramel to cool. You should hear it start to crack, which is what it is supposed to do.

Directions for Custard
Add 3 whole eggs and 2 yolks to a mixing bowl; beat together with a wire whisk or fork. Add evaporated milk, condensed milk, and sugar to the eggs; beat again until well combined. (You may pour mixture through a strainer if

HOW TO SWAP BATCHES OF COOKIES AND CANDY WITH OTHERS

you feel it is needed.) Pour this mixture into the caramelized bowl. Place the bowl in a baking pan deep enough to add about 2 or 3 inches to make a water bath for the Flan. Place in an oven preheated to 350° F and bake for 1 hour. Insert knife in the center to check for doneness. If the knife comes out clean, the Flan is done. Let cool before refrigerating to chill completely. Invert the bowl onto a serving platter with edges deep enough to contain the caramel sauce. The caramel will dissolve into a nice thick sauce after the custard has set in the bowl in the refrigerator during the chilling process. Pour the caramel sauce in the serving dish to enjoy with the Flan. Enjoy.

Eggs

KATHERINE W. MASHBURN

FLUFFY ICE CREAM FROSTY
From the Kitchen of Brenda Blaylock

Ingredients
1 can of Eagle Brand condensed milk
1 – 16 oz. container of cool whip
Chocolate milk

Directions
Put all ingredients in an ice cream maker and mix just as you do for ice cream. Do not freeze it hard. It should be fluffy like a Wendy's frosty. Enjoy.

HOW TO SWAP BATCHES OF COOKIES AND CANDY WITH OTHERS

GLAZED CHERRY CREAM CHEESE DANISH

From the Kitchen of Kathy Mashburn

Ingredients
2 packages crescent rolls
2 – 8 oz. packages cream cheese
1 cup sugar, plus 1 tablespoon
1 egg
1 teaspoon vanilla
1 egg white, beaten
1 can of cherry pie filling (or any other flavor)

Directions
Spray a 9x13 inch baking pan with non-stick cooking spray. Roll the first can of crescent rolls into the baking pan. Using your fingers, press the seams together. Combine cream cheese, egg, and sugar until smooth and pour over the crescent rolls. Spread pie filling over top of the cream cheese mixture. (For plain cream cheese Danish, omit the pie filling.) Roll out the second can of crescent rolls and use to cover cream cheese and pie filling. Brush the dough with egg white and sprinkle with a tablespoon of granulated sugar. Bake at 350° F for 25 minutes or until golden brown.

Ingredients and Directions for Glaze
½ cup powdered sugar
½ teaspoon vanilla
2 tablespoons milk

KATHERINE W. MASHBURN

Mix ingredients well; spread over top of slightly warm Danish. Enjoy.

Cherries

GRANNY'S COBBLER
From the Kitchen of Mary Coker

Ingredients
1 stick butter, melted
1 cup sugar
Any prepared or sliced fruit (apples, peaches, pears, strawberries, etc.)
1 can of Pet evaporated milk
2 cans canned biscuits, or homemade biscuits

Directions
Place fruit in a casserole baking dish. Cover with melted butter, sugar, and evaporated milk before randomly placing biscuits on top. Brush top of the biscuits with melted butter and sprinkle with sugar. Bake at 350° F until done. Enjoy.

Raisins

GRANNY BROWN'S MONKEY BREAD
From the Kitchen of Nan D. Brown and Natalie Smith

Ingredients
4 cans of refrigerated biscuits (40)
1 ½ teaspoons cinnamon
½ cup butter
1 cup white sugar
1 cup brown sugar
½ cup pecans, raisins, or coconut (optional)

Directions
Cut each biscuit into 4 pieces. Place white sugar and cinnamon into a plastic bag; add biscuit pieces a few at a time and shake to coat. Place coated pieces in a greased tube pan until all pieces are used. Sprinkle layers with pecans, raisins, or coconut, if desired. In a saucepan, bring brown sugar and butter to a boil. Pour over top of the biscuits. Bake at 350° F for 45 minutes. Allow to cool 15 minutes before removing from the pan. Invert onto serving platter. Pieces can be picked apart or bread can be sliced to serve. Enjoy.

KATHERINE W. MASHBURN

Oranges

HEAVENLY ORANGE CHEESECAKE
From the Kitchen of Linda Allen

Ingredients
1 cup graham cracker crumbs
1/3 cup butter, melted
24 oz. cream cheese, softened
1 cup sugar
1/3 cup heavy whipping cream
½ cup fresh squeezed orange juice
Zest from 1 orange
4 eggs
¼ teaspoon orange extract
½ teaspoon vanilla extract

Directions
Preheat oven to 300° F. In a medium bowl, mix together graham cracker crumbs and melted butter. Press moist crumbs into the bottom of a 10 inch spring form pan; set aside. In a large bowl, mix cream cheese and sugar until smooth and creamy. Add eggs one at a time; mixing well after each addition. Add in orange juice, heavy cream, zest, and extracts; stir until well blended. Bake for 1 hour; turn oven off, but leave cheesecake in the oven for 15 to 20

HOW TO SWAP BATCHES OF
COOKIES AND CANDY WITH OTHERS

minutes longer without opening the door. Remove from oven and allow cooling to room temperature before placing in the refrigerator to cool completely. Loosen the sides of the cheesecake from the pan. Spread top of the cheesecake with Orange Zest frosting.

Ingredients and Directions for Orange Zest Frosting
1 cup low-fat Greek style yogurt or sour cream
½ cup powdered milk
2 teaspoons orange zest
¼ teaspoon orange extract

Combine ingredients for frosting; mix well. Spread on top of cheesecake. Enjoy.

Frost

KATHERINE W. MASHBURN

Graham Crackers

ICE CREAM PIE
From the Kitchen of Natalie Smith

Ingredients
2 cups cold milk
1 ½ cups vanilla ice cream, softened
2 packages (4 oz. each) Jell-O chocolate instant pudding mix
1 – 6 oz. graham cracker crust

Directions
Pour milk into a large bowl and add ice cream and dry pudding mixes; beat with wire whisk until well blended. Let stand 5 minutes or until mixture is very thick and will mound. Spoon mixture into graham cracker crust and refrigerate for 4 hours or overnight until set. Enjoy.

HOW TO SWAP BATCHES OF
COOKIES AND CANDY WITH OTHERS

IMPOSSIBLE PIE
From the Kitchen of Darlene Lucas

Ingredients
4 eggs, beaten
1 ½ cups sugar
2 cups milk
½ cup self-rising flour
1 teaspoon vanilla extract
½ stick butter or margarine, melted
1 – 7 oz. package of coconut, flaked

Directions
Blend eggs and sugar, and then add flour and other ingredients. Bake in greased pans at 350° F for 30 minutes. NOTE: This pie makes its own crust. Enjoy.

Coconut

KATHERINE W. MASHBURN

JELL-O PIES
From the Kitchen of Darlene Lucas

Ingredients
1 cup sugar
1 ½ cups pineapple juice
1 small package strawberry Jell-O
1 Large can of evaporated milk (cold)
1 box Vanilla wafer cookies

Directions
Refrigerate milk overnight, if possible. The colder it is, the better it whips up. Line 2 - 9 inch pie pans with vanilla wafers in the bottom and around the sides.

In a medium saucepan, mix sugar and pineapple juice; bring to a boil. Remove from heat and add dry Jell-O; mix well and set aside to cool.

In a large (chilled) mixing bowl, beat milk on high speed with an electric mixer. It should double in volume. Beat 2 to 3 minutes reducing amount of air bubbles in milk. Reduce mixer to low and slowly pour in Jell-O mixture; blend or stir until mixed well.

Pour into vanilla wafer crusts; chill 3 to 4 hours or overnight before serving. NOTE: Substitute other flavors of graham cracker crusts and Jell-O that will blend well with pineapple flavor. Enjoy.

HOW TO SWAP BATCHES OF
COOKIES AND CANDY WITH OTHERS

JOY CAKE
From the Kitchen of Cindy McEntyre

Ingredients
Frozen coconut (I use the Tropical Isle brand for its moistness.)
Pecans
1 German Chocolate cake mix
1 stick butter
1 – 8 oz. package cream cheese
1 box 10X confectioner sugar

Directions
Grease and flour a 9x13 inch cake pan or spray with non-stick cooking spray to skip flouring. Spread 3 ½ oz. coconut and 1 cup pecans in the bottom of pan or use 6 oz. unthawed coconut to spread over the bottom of pan using your hands; sprinkle about ½ cup of pecans over coconut.

Prepare the German Chocolate cake mix according to directions on the package. Pour cake batter over the coconut and pecan mixture.

Melt butter and cream with cream cheese. Add in the powdered sugar; mix well.

Drop by tablespoonfuls onto top of cake batter. Continue dropping spoonfuls until mixture is used up. It doesn't matter if they overlap. Cover as much of the cake top as possible. The mixture will sink down into the cake as it bakes and rises. Bake at 350° F for 45 to 55 minutes until cake pulls away from the sides of the pan. Enjoy.

KEY LIME CAKE
From the Kitchen of Renee Baynes

Ingredients
Butter for greasing pan
Flour for dusting pan
1 – 3 oz. package lime flavored gelatin
1 1/3 cups granulated sugar
2 cups all-purpose flour, sifted
½ teaspoon salt
1 teaspoon baking powder
1 teaspoon baking soda
1 ½ cups vegetable oil
¾ cup orange juice
1 tablespoon lemon juice
½ cup vanilla extract
5 large eggs, slightly beaten

Ingredients for Glaze
½ cup key lime juice (from about 25 small key limes or 4 large regular limes)
½ cup confectioner sugar

Ingredients for Icing
½ cup (1 stick) butter, softened to room temperature
1 – 8 oz. package cream cheese, softened
1 – 1 lb. box confectioner sugar

HOW TO SWAP BATCHES OF COOKIES AND CANDY WITH OTHERS

Directions

For the Cake: Preheat oven to 350° F; grease and flour a 9x12x2 cake pan. In a large mixing bowl, mix gelatin, granulated sugar, flour, salt, baking powder, and baking soda; stir to mix well. Add oil, orange juice, lemon juice, vanilla, and eggs; mix again until combined well. Pour the batter evenly into pan and bake for 35 to 40 minutes.

For the Glaze: While the cake is still hot, mix the lime juice and confectioners' sugar together well. Pierce the cake with a fork to allow the glaze to soak in better and pour it over the cake. Allow cake to cool completely as you prepare the icing.

For the Icing: Cream butter and cream cheese together; beat in the confectioners' sugar until the mixture is smooth and easy to spread over cake. Enjoy.

KATHERINE W. MASHBURN

LEMONADE PIE
From the Kitchen of Rachel Morehead

Ingredients
1 – 8 oz. container cool whip, thawed
1 can of Eagle Brand condensed milk
1 – 6 oz. can of frozen lemonade, thawed
1 graham cracker crust

Directions
Mix together the cool whip, condensed milk, and frozen lemonade; pour into graham cracker crust. Allow pie to set overnight. NOTE: I have used frozen limeade and it is just as good. Also, if a 6 oz. can of frozen lemonade is not available, use half of a 12 oz. can and make lemonade with the remainder. Enjoy.

I Love Baking

HOW TO SWAP BATCHES OF
COOKIES AND CANDY WITH OTHERS

LUSCIOUS KEY LIME CAKE
From the Kitchen Brenda Blaylock

Ingredients
1 box Duncan Hines Moist Deluxe Lemon Supreme cake mix
1 small package instant lemon pudding and pie filling
4 eggs
1 cup Crisco oil
¾ cup water
¼ cup of key lime or lime juice

Ingredients and Directions for Glaze
2 ¼ cups confectioner sugar, divided
1/3 cup key lime juice
1 tablespoon water
2 tablespoons butter or margarine, melted
Lime or strawberry slices for garnish (optional)
Prepare glaze by combining confectioner sugar, key lime juice, water, and melted butter in a medium bowl.

Directions
Preheat oven to 350° F. Grease and flour a 10 inch Bundt pan.

For cake: combine cake mix, instant pudding mix, eggs, oil, water, and ¼ cup key lime juice in large bowl; beat at medium speed with electric mixer for 2 minutes. Pour batter into Bundt pan. Bake at 350° F for 50 to 60 minutes or until toothpick inserted in center comes out clean. Cool cake in Bundt pan for 25 minutes before inverting onto a cooling rack. Return cake to the pan and poke holes in the top of the warm cake using a skewer or long-pronged fork. Slowly pour the glaze over the cake. Cool cake completely before inverting it again onto a serving plate. Dust with confectioner sugar and garnish with lime slices or strawberries, if desired. Enjoy.

I
Love
Baking

HOW TO SWAP BATCHES OF
COOKIES AND CANDY WITH OTHERS

MAMOW EDNA'S 'REAL GOOD' CAKE
From the Kitchen of Yvette Dunn

Ingredients
1 cup sugar
2 tablespoon butter
½ cup sweet milk
1 cup plain all-purpose flour
2 teaspoons baking powder
¼ teaspoon salt
1/3 cup cocoa, plus 2 tablespoons cocoa
½ to ¾ cup of nuts, chopped
1 ½ cups of boiling water

Directions
Preheat oven to 350° F and spray a 9 inch square baking pan with non-stick cooking spray. Cream together ¾ cup of sugar and butter; stir in sweet milk. Sift together plain flour, baking powder, salt, and 2 tablespoons cocoa. Add dry ingredients to the sugar and butter mixture; mix until smooth. Add chopped nuts, if desired. Pour batter into prepared pan.

In a separate bowl, mix together the other ½ cup sugar and 1/3 cup cocoa. Sprinkle over top of cake batter already in the pan; pour boiling water over the top of the batter. Bake cake at 350° F for 35 to 40 minutes.

As the cake bakes, the bottom will rise to the top. The water and sugar will make rich chocolate syrup in the bottom. Enjoy.

KATHERINE W. MASHBURN

MISSISSIPPI MUD CAKE
From the Kitchen of Cindy McEntyre

Ingredients
1/3 cup cocoa
2 sticks butter (1/2 lb.)
1 cup pecan pieces
4 eggs
2 cups sugar
1 cup coconut, flaked
1 ½ cups plain flour
1 small jar marshmallow cream

Directions
Combine all the above ingredients (except marshmallow cream); mix well. Butter a 9x13 baking pan; pour batter into pan and bake at 350° F for 30 minutes. As soon as you remove cake from the oven, spread with marshmallow cream and allow the cake to cool in the pan.

Ingredients and Directions for Icing
1 stick butter
6 tablespoons milk (may add a little more depending on consistency of the icing)
3 tablespoons cocoa
1 box 10X confectioner sugar
1 cup pecan pieces
1 teaspoon vanilla extract
1 cup coconut, flaked

Bring butter, milk, and cocoa to a boil. Remove from heat being sure all cocoa lumps are gone. Add confectioner sugar and mix well. Add remaining ingredients; mix well. Spread icing over the marshmallow cream on the cake. NOTE: If icing is too thick to spread easily, add 2 tablespoons of milk at a time until it reaches spreading consistency. Enjoy.

MOMMA'S COCONUT CREAM CAKE
From the Kitchen of Nita Cochran and Natalie Smith

Ingredients
1 package Duncan Hines white cake mix
1 can of Cream of Coconut
1 can of Eagle Brand Condensed Milk
1 – 8 oz. container of cool whip
2 packages of frozen coconut

Directions
Prepare cake mix as directed on the package; bake in a 9x13 inch pan. While the cake is warm, punch holes in it with a fork or straw. Mix together cream of coconut and condensed milk. Pour mixture evenly over the cake before spreading cool whip evenly over the mixture. Enjoy.

KATHERINE W. MASHBURN

MOUNTAIN DEW APPLE CAKE
From the Kitchen of Elizabeth Fielden

Ingredients
2 sticks butter, melted
2 cups sugar
1 ½ cups Mountain Dew soda
2 Granny Smith apples cut into ½ inch slices
2 cans crescent rolls

Directions
Melt butter and sugar together; mix well. Slice apples into ½ inch pieces. Wrap a crescent roll triangle around each slice of apple. Arrange wrapped apples in 9x13 inch baking dish. Slowly pour the butter mixture over the apples, and then pour the Mountain Dew soda over the top. Bake at 350° F for 40 to 45 minutes. Enjoy.

Apples

HOW TO SWAP BATCHES OF
COOKIES AND CANDY WITH OTHERS

MRS. 'BUCK' BRACKET POUND CAKE

From the Kitchen of Yvette Dunn

Ingredients

5 eggs, at room temperature
3 cups plain flour, sifted
3 cups sugar
2 sticks butter, softened to room temperature
½ cup Crisco
½ teaspoon baking powder
¼ teaspoon salt
1 cup sweet milk
1 teaspoon vanilla flavoring
1 teaspoon lemon flavoring

Directions

Cream together butter, Crisco, and sugar until light and fluffy (about 10 minutes). Add eggs one at a time; beat well after each addition. Add mixed dry ingredients alternately with milk; beating after each addition. Add vanilla and lemon flavorings. Pour batter into a tube pan that has been well greased with Crisco and floured. Bake the cake at 325° F for 1 ½ hours or until toothpick inserted in the center comes out clean. (DO NOT OPEN OVEN DOOR.) Remove from oven and place right-side up on a wire rack; allow cooling for 15 to 20 minutes. Turn cake out of pan onto serving platter to cool completely. Enjoy.

KATHERINE W. MASHBURN

ORANGESICLE CUPCAKES
From the Kitchen of Sabrina Gail Owens

Ingredients and Directions for Cupcakes
½ cup butter, softened
1 cup shortening
2 cups granulated sugar
4 large eggs
3 cups cake flour or sifted all-purpose flour
2 teaspoons baking powder
½ teaspoon salt
1 cup buttermilk
1 teaspoon vanilla extract
1 tablespoon orange juice
1 tablespoon orange zest

Cream together butter and shortening until completely mixed. Cream in sugar; beat in eggs one at a time. Combine the dry ingredients, while alternately adding buttermilk. Stir in vanilla, orange juice, and zest. Pour batter into lined muffin pans and bake at 350° F for about 20 to 25 minutes until golden brown or until toothpick inserted in the center comes out clean. Allow cupcakes to cool.

Ingredients and Directions for Orange Frosting
½ cup butter, softened
½ cup shortening
2 teaspoons orange juice
1 ½ teaspoons orange zest
½ teaspoon vanilla extract

HOW TO SWAP BATCHES OF COOKIES AND CANDY WITH OTHERS

4-5 cups powdered sugar
2 drops orange food coloring
Orange sprinkles or Orange candy slices for garnish

Cream butter and shortening; add orange juice, zest, and vanilla. Beat in powdered sugar until frosting reaches a spreading consistency. Add drops of food coloring until frosting is a color you like. Spread or pipe frosting onto cooled cupcakes. Use sprinkles or orange candy pieces to garnish, if desired. Enjoy.

Oranges

KATHERINE W. MASHBURN

ORANGE JUICE CAKE
From the Kitchen of Polly Jones

Ingredients
1 box Duncan Hines cake mix
1 small box instant vanilla pudding
1 cup oil
1 cup orange juice with lots of pulp
4 eggs
½ cup chopped nuts

Directions
Place nuts in the bottom of a greased Bundt pan. Mix all ingredients and pour batter over chopped nuts. Bake at 350° F for approximately 45 minutes or until toothpick inserted in the center comes out clean. When the cake is nearing done make the glaze listed below.

Ingredients and Directions for Glaze
1 stick butter
1/3 cup orange juice
1 ¼ cup sugar
Zest or grated peel from 1 orange

In a saucepan, mix all ingredients and bring to a boil for 2 minutes on the stovetop. Slowly pour glaze over the cake while it is still hot and while it is still in the pan. Allow the cake to stay in the pan for at least 30 minutes before inverting it onto a serving platter. NOTE: This cake will disappear quickly, so watch it closely. Enjoy.

HOW TO SWAP BATCHES OF
COOKIES AND CANDY WITH OTHERS

PEACH COBBLER
From the Kitchen of Brooke Keeler

Ingredients
2 ½ cups sweetened peaches with juice
1 stick butter
1 cup sugar
1 cup milk
1 cup self-rising flour

Directions
Pour peaches into bottom of 9x13 inch baking dish. Melt butter; pour over the peaches. In a medium bowl, mix sugar, flour, and milk. Pour this batter over the top of the peaches and melted butter. Bake at 350° F for 30 to 40 minutes until the crust is golden brown. NOTE: I like to add a little more sugar to the top of the cobbler halfway through the baking process to make it a little sweeter. Enjoy.

Peaches

KATHERINE W. MASHBURN

All-purpose Flour

PEANUT BUTTER CAKE
From the Kitchen of Linda Allen

Ingredients and Directions for Cake
2 cups all-purpose flour
1/3 cup cocoa
2 teaspoons baking powder
1 teaspoon baking soda
¼ teaspoon salt
2 cups sugar
3 eggs
2 teaspoons vanilla extract
1 cup of butter (2 sticks), melted and cooled to room temperature
1 cup buttermilk

Preheat oven to 350° F and spray 2 – 9 inch baking pans with non-stick cooking spray; set aside.

In a large bowl, mix together the flour, cocoa, baking powder, baking soda, salt, and sugar with a whisk. In a separate smaller bowl, mix together the butter, vanilla extract, eggs, and buttermilk. Pour the liquid mixture into the flour mixture and stir until moistened. Divide the batter

HOW TO SWAP BATCHES OF COOKIES AND CANDY WITH OTHERS

into the pans and bake for 25 to 30 minutes or until a toothpick inserted in the center comes out clean. Allow cakes to cool in the pans for 10 minutes; remove them from the pans onto a wire rack to cool completely.

Place one layer of cake on a serving plate and cover completely with peanut butter frosting. Top with the other cake layer; spread the sides and top of the cake with frosting. Using the remaining frosting, pipe a border around the edges of the cake. Cut the peanut butter cups into pieces and place around the sides of the cake. Use a few whole peanut butter cups on top of cake to garnish. Place the frosted cake in the refrigerator or freezer until the frosting becomes firm. NOTE: Both white and chocolate cake mixes work great in this recipe.

Ingredients and Directions for Frosting
1 – 8 oz. package of cream cheese, softened
½ cup creamy peanut butter
1 teaspoon vanilla extract
2/3 cup powdered sugar
1 large container cool whip or whipped topping
1 package of small peanut butter cups

In a medium bowl, whip cream cheese, peanut butter, and vanilla extract together until smooth and creamy. Add powdered sugar; mix thoroughly. Fold in whipped topping. Enjoy.

KATHERINE W. MASHBURN

Peanut Butter

PEANUT BUTTER PIE
From the Kitchen of Brandi Nagy

Ingredients
1 small bag of Reeses cups
9 oz. cool whip
1 - 8 oz. package cream cheese (softened to room temperature)
1 cup creamy peanut butter
1 cup confectioner sugar
1 graham cracker crust

Directions
Place cool whip, cream cheese, peanut butter, and sugar in a medium sized mixing bowl; mix well until there are no chunks. The mixture should be a pale tan color. Pour the mixture into the graham cracker crust; chop Reese cups into small pieces and sprinkle on top of the pie. Refrigerate until cool and firm. Enjoy.

HOW TO SWAP BATCHES OF
COOKIES AND CANDY WITH OTHERS

Pies

PEANUT BUTTER PIE
From the Kitchen of Kathryn Owens

Ingredients

1 – 8 oz. package cream cheese
1 – 16 oz. container cool whip
1 ½ cups peanut butter
1 ½ cups powdered sugar
2 chocolate pie crusts or regular graham cracker crusts

Directions

Using a spoon, mix all ingredients well. It will be thick. Divide and pour into the chocolate pie crusts or graham cracker crusts. Refrigerate until ready to serve. Pies must be kept cool, otherwise they will melt. Enjoy.

KATHERINE W. MASHBURN

PECAN COBBLER
From the Kitchen of Renee Baynes

Ingredients for Crust
1 ½ cups of all-purpose flour
1 tablespoon granulated sugar
½ teaspoon sea salt
1 ½ teaspoons baking powder
4 tablespoons (½ stick) butter, chilled
½ cup half and half

Ingredients for Filling
4 large eggs
2 tablespoons half and half
¾ cup brown sugar
3 tablespoons (½ stick) butter, melted
1 cup sorghum syrup (may substitute dark Karo syrup)
¼ teaspoon sea salt
½ teaspoon vanilla extract
1 ½ cups pecan halves

Directions
Preheat oven to 350° F and grease a 9x9 inch baking dish or a large cast iron skillet. Mix together flour, sugar, salt, and baking powder. Cut chilled butter into pieces and work it into the flour mixture with your hands or a pastry blender until it resembles pea-sized crumbs. Stir in the half and half; mix until it is a bit smooth and sticky. Pour dough out onto a floured surface and knead for 1 minute. Roll the dough out to a 1/8 inch thickness; press it into the bottom of the baking dish or skillet.

HOW TO SWAP BATCHES OF COOKIES AND CANDY WITH OTHERS

Combine eggs, half and half, and brown sugar; mix until well blended. Stir in melted butter, syrup, salt, and vanilla extract; mixing again until well blended. Place pecans on top of crust; pour filling over it. Bake uncovered for 40 to 45 minutes or until the custard (filling) is set. NOTE: Don't forget to serve with a big scoop of vanilla bean ice cream on top. Enjoy.

Cobblers

KATHERINE W. MASHBURN

PINA COLADA CAKE
From the Kitchen of Mary Coker

Ingredients
1 box of Pineapple cake mix
1 can of Eagle Brand condensed milk
1 bag shredded coconut
Fresh cherries (or from a jar, drained)
1 can of Pina Colada drink mix
1 – 16 oz. container cool whip

Directions
Prepare cake as directed on the box; bake in a 9x13 inch glass baking dish. Using the handle of a wooden spoon, poke holes in the cake layer after it has cooled slightly. Mix together Pina Colada drink mix and condensed milk; pour over cake. Allow mixture to soak into poked holes. Spread crushed pineapple over cake, and then add cool whip on top. Sprinkle coconut over cool whip. Garnish with cherries, if desired. Keep cake refrigerated until ready to serve. Enjoy.

Pineapple

HOW TO SWAP BATCHES OF
COOKIES AND CANDY WITH OTHERS

PINEAPPLE AND BLUEBERRY CAKE
From the Kitchen of Diane Bean

Ingredients
1 can of pineapple in heavy syrup, crushed
1 bag of blueberries
1 box Butter flavored cake mix
1 cup and a ½ cup powdered sugar
1 cup pecans
1 cup butter, melted

Directions
In a 9x13 inch baking pan, layer ingredients in this order: pineapple, blueberries, powdered sugar, Butter cake mix, and pecans. Pour melted butter over cake mix, and then sprinkle cup of powdered sugar on top. Bake at 350° F for 20 minutes. Enjoy.

Cakes

KATHERINE W. MASHBURN

PLAIN CHEESECAKE
From the Kitchen of Kathy Mashburn

Ingredients and Directions for Crust
1 – 9 inch spring form pan
1 ¾ cups crushed vanilla wafer cookies
¼ cup sugar
½ teaspoon of cinnamon
½ cup melted butter

Combine the above ingredients; mix well. Press into bottom of pan and about halfway up the side of the pan. Do not bake crust yet.

Ingredients and Directions for Filling
2 teaspoons vanilla extract
3 eggs
3 – 8 oz. packages of cream cheese (softened)
1 ¼ cup sugar
1 cup sour cream
Preheat oven to 350° F. Blend cream cheese and sugar together well. Add in eggs one at a time; beating mixture after each egg. Add sour cream and vanilla extract. Pour filling into the pan and bake cheesecake for 1 hour. When baking time has lapsed, turn off oven and leave cheesecake inside for another 45 minutes to an hour. Serve plain or with any flavor pie filling or topping like strawberry, peach, apple or blueberry. Enjoy.

HOW TO SWAP BATCHES OF
COOKIES AND CANDY WITH OTHERS

POPCORN CAKE
From the Kitchen of Cindy Ownby

Ingredients
1 package of miniature marshmallows
½ cup butter
10 cups popped popcorn
1 ½ cups of salted peanuts
1 cup M&M candies

Directions
Melt the marshmallows and butter in a heavy saucepan. Place the popcorn in a large mixing bowl, and pour the marshmallow mixture over it; mix well. Stir in peanuts and M&M candies. Press into a 10 inch greased Bundt pan; cool until firm. Remove from pan and cut into desired size slices with a serrated knife. Enjoy.

POPCORN CEREAL
From the Kitchen of Esperanza Reyes

Ingredients
3 cups regular popcorn, popped
½ cup brown sugar
Milk

Directions
Pour popped corn into a small bowl; remove un-popped kernels. Sprinkle with brown sugar and serve with cold milk. Enjoy.

KATHERINE W. MASHBURN

PUMPKIN ROLL
From the Kitchen of Elizabeth Fielden

Ingredients and Directions for Roll
2/3 cup pumpkin (for pies)
¾ cup self-rising flour
3 eggs
1 cup sugar
1 teaspoon cinnamon

Mix the above ingredients together. Spray a baking sheet with non-stick cooking spray like Pam. Lay a piece of wax paper over the sprayed baking sheet; pour batter into the pan. Bake at 350° F for about 18 minutes or until toothpick inserted into the center comes out clean. Sprinkle a clean dish towel with granulated sugar. Turn out roll-up from the pan and onto the towel. Roll it up with the wax paper still attached until cool.

Ingredients and Directions for Filling and Icing
1 cup powdered sugar
1 – 8 oz. package cream cheese
3 teaspoons butter, melted
1 teaspoon vanilla flavoring
Pecan pieces or halves to garnish

Mix the above ingredients well; spread onto the flattened roll you would have unrolled from the towel after it had cooled. Re-roll again using the wax paper (jelly-roll style). Spread remaining cream cheese frosting on the top and sprinkle with pecan pieces, or place halves down the center

HOW TO SWAP BATCHES OF COOKIES AND CANDY WITH OTHERS

of the roll to garnish. Keep the roll refrigerated until ready to serve. Enjoy.

Cinnamon

KATHERINE W. MASHBURN

ROBERTA'S CAKE
From the Kitchen of Elizabeth Fielden

Ingredients and Directions for Cake
1 box Swiss Chocolate cake mix
1 small box instant vanilla pudding mix
1 ½ cups of milk
1 cup oil
3 eggs

Preheat oven to 350° F and grease or spray with non-stick cooking spray 2 - 9 inch cake pans. Combine all ingredients; mix until well blended. Divide and pour batter into pans; bake for 20 to 25 minutes or until toothpick inserted in center comes out clean. Allow cake to cool.

Ingredients and Directions for Icing
1 – 8 oz. package cream cheese
1 – 16 oz. container cool whip
1 cup powdered sugar
½ cup granulated sugar
1 King size Hersey candy bar, grated

Combine above ingredients, except grated chocolate; mix until well blended. Fold in grated chocolate. Use plenty of frosting between layers and on sides and top when frosting cake. Refrigerate to chill before serving. Enjoy.

HOW TO SWAP BATCHES OF
COOKIES AND CANDY WITH OTHERS

SIMPLE CHEESECAKE
From the Kitchen of Melinda Williams

Ingredients
1 graham cracker crust
1 – 8 oz. package cream cheese, softened
1 – 8 oz. container sour cream
1 teaspoon vanilla extract
1 cup sugar
1 – 8 oz. container cool whip

Directions
Mix all ingredients well; pour into pie crust. Refrigerate to chill. Garnish with fresh fruit or any flavor of pie filling before serving. Enjoy.

KATHERINE W. MASHBURN

SNOW CAKE
From the Kitchen of Elizabeth Fielden

Ingredients and Directions for Cake
1 box yellow cake mix
¾ cup vegetable oil
4 eggs
1 – 11 oz. can mandarin oranges and juice
1 cup chopped pecans

Lightly grease and flour 3 – 8 inch cake pans; set aside. Combine the above ingredients in a large mixing bowl; blend until moistened. Using a mixer beat on medium speed for 40 minutes. Divide and spread batter evenly in prepared pans. Bake at 350° F for 20 to 25 minutes or until toothpick inserted in the center comes out clean. Allow cakes to cool completely.

Ingredients and Directions for Icing
1 cup powdered sugar
1 – 8 oz. can crushed pineapple (do not drain)
1 – 8 oz. container cool whip
1 – 8 oz. container sour cream

Combine the above ingredients in a large mixing bowl; blend together by hand. Spread frosting between the layers of cake as you stack them on a serving plate. Completely cover the sides and top of the cake with frosting. Refrigerate the cake immediately. Garnish with mandarin oranges or pecans before serving, if desired. Enjoy.

HOW TO SWAP BATCHES OF
COOKIES AND CANDY WITH OTHERS

Sour Cream

SOUR CREAM COCONUT CAKE
From the Kitchen of Cindy McEntyre

Ingredients and Directions for Cake Filling (to be made a day ahead)
1 small package frozen coconut, thawed
1 – 8 oz. container sour cream
2 cups sugar

Mix together the filling ingredients using a spoon; store overnight in the refrigerator.

Ingredients and Directions for Cake
1 box yellow Butter recipe cake mix

Prepare cake as directed on the box. Bake in 2 – 9 inch round cake pans. Do not over bake. Cool layers on a wire rack. After the cake has completely cooled, split each layer in half to make a total of 4 thin layers. TIP: This can be done using a special baking wire or dental floss. Spread filling between all layers as you stack them on a serving plate. If there is leftover filling, poke holes in the top layer and spread the filling on the top. IMPORTANT TIP: Turn the cut sides of all layers up as you stack them, except for the top layer, which should be placed cut side down. This allows the filling to better saturate the cake for moistness.

Ingredients and Directions for Frosting
1 – 16 oz. container cool whip (or 2 – 8 oz. containers), thawed
1 small package frozen coconut, thawed
Mix the cool whip and coconut together lightly; spread frosting on top and around the sides thickly sealing the edges of the cake. Sprinkle additional coconut on top, if desired. Store cake covered in the refrigerator for at least 1 day before serving. The cake will become very moist. This cake will keep for several days in the refrigerator. Recipe yields a very large cake with 10 to 12 servings. Enjoy.

Refrigerate

HOW TO SWAP BATCHES OF
COOKIES AND CANDY WITH OTHERS

SOUTHERN SWEET CITRUS POUND CAKE
From the Kitchen of Darlene Lucas

Ingredients and Directions for Cake
3 cups flour (I prefer cake flour)
2 sticks butter
½ cup shortening
3 cups sugar
5 eggs
½ teaspoon vanilla extract
1 teaspoon lemon extract (I prefer to add zest of a ½ lemon)
6 oz. of any citrus flavored soda

Cream butter and shortening together in a large mixing bowl. Gradually add sugar; mix well. If you add all the sugar at once it will be extremely hard to mix. Add 1 egg at a time and gradually add the flour to the mix in between the eggs; beating the mixture well after each egg. After all ingredients have been mixed well, add the vanilla and lemon (or zest) extracts; mix well. Pour batter into a greased and floured Bundt pan. Bake at 325° F for 1 hour and 15 minutes. Remove from oven and allow cooling; invert onto a serving plate. Drizzle with icing while slightly warm. Enjoy.

Ingredients and Directions for Icing
2 cups confectioner sugar
2 tablespoons butter, melted (I add the zest of ½ lemon)
2 oz. citrus flavored soda

Mix together the above ingredients; drizzle over cake while it is still warm. Enjoy.

STRAWBERRY DAIQUIRI CAKE
From the Kitchen of Mary Coker

Ingredients
1 box Strawberry cake mix
1 bottle Daiquiri mix
1 can of Eagle Brand condensed milk
2 cans strawberry pie filling
1 – 16 oz. container cool whip
Fresh or frozen strawberries for garnish

Directions
Prepare cake as directed on box and bake in a 9x13 baking dish. Using the handle of a wooden spoon, poke holes in the cake after it has cooled slightly. Mix the strawberry daiquiri mix and condensed milk together; pour over cake allowing it to soak into the poked holes. Spread strawberry pie filling over the top of the daiquiri mixture, and then cover with cool whip. Garnish with strawberries, if desired. Store the cake in refrigerator until ready to serve. Enjoy.

HOW TO SWAP BATCHES OF
COOKIES AND CANDY WITH OTHERS

STRAWBERRY PECAN BREAD

From the Kitchen of Elizabeth Fielden

Ingredients
1 cup fresh strawberries, washed and sliced
1 ½ cups self-rising flour
1 cup granulated sugar, plus 2 tablespoons
1 tablespoon ground cinnamon (or 1 teaspoon, if less is preferred)
½ cup vegetable oil
2 eggs, beaten
1 cup chopped pecans or walnuts (optional)

Directions
Place strawberries in a small bowl and sprinkle 2 tablespoons sugar over them; stir and set aside. In a mixing bowl, combine flour, sugar, oil, eggs, cinnamon; mix until well blended. Stir in strawberries and nuts; mix again until well blended. The batter should be a pretty shade of pink. Pour batter into a greased and floured loaf pan. Bake at 350° F for 45 to 50 minutes or until toothpick inserted in the center comes out clean. Allow bread to cool in pan for 10 minutes before inverting on a serving platter; cool completely. NOTES: For an extra special treat, toast and butter a slice or spread with cream cheese before serving. This recipe yields 1 regular-sized loaf. Recipe also works well using peaches. If bread seems doughy after specified baking time, add increments of 5 minutes additional time until the bread is done. Approximate baking time for mini-loafs and regular-sized muffins is 30 minutes, and 25 minutes for mini-muffins. Enjoy.

KATHERINE W. MASHBURN

SUGAR-FREE DOUBLE DARK CHOCOLATE CAKE
From the Kitchen of Linda Allen

Ingredients and Directions for Cake
1 package sugar-free brownie mix
2 cups all-purpose flour
1 ½ teaspoon baking powder
¼ teaspoon salt
1 ½ cups Splenda artificial sweetener
3 eggs
½ cup oil
1 ½ cups of water

Directions
Preheat oven to 350° F and spray 3 - 9 inch baking pans with non-stick cooking spray; set aside.

In large bowl, combine flour, brownie mix, baking powder, salt, and artificial sweetener. Add eggs, oil, and water; mix on medium speed for 2 minutes. Divide batter into pans; bake for 20 to 25 minutes or until toothpick inserted in the center comes out clean. Cool in pans for 10 minutes before removing to wire racks; cool completely. Spread the ganache between the layers as you stack them on a serving plate.

Ingredients and Directions for Dark Chocolate Ganache Filling
16 oz. dark chocolate chips
1/3 cup heavy cream

HOW TO SWAP BATCHES OF COOKIES AND CANDY WITH OTHERS

4 tablespoons Agave nectar
3 tablespoons butter

In a microwaveable bowl, combine all ingredients and put in microwave on defrost setting for 90 seconds; stir until smooth and creamy. Allow ganache to cool, stirring until it becomes spreadable. Spread ganache between the layers of the cake as you stack them. Repeat the same recipe for ganache, but this time pour it over top of the cake and spread it around the sides before it thickens and cools. Allow the cake to sit for a while for the ganache to set. Enjoy.

Dark Chocolate

CONCLUSION

I truly hope you have enjoyed learning about swapping batches of cookies and candy with others. A well planned Batch-Swap will result in an array of delicious cookies and candy for all participates. They're excellent opportunities to share laughter and good times with your favorite people. The time you spend fellowshipping with others will be much sweeter than all the cookies and candy in the world.

This book has been a true joy to write. Thanks again to everyone who shared recipes to make this book possible.

Happy Swapping!

Kathy

www.kathymashburnbooks.com

HOW TO SWAP BATCHES OF COOKIES AND CANDY WITH OTHERS

INDEX

Cookies and Candy	*Page*
A Favorite Candy	33
Baker's One Bowl Chocolate Bliss Cookies	34
Black Bean Brownies	35,36
Blonde Brownies	36
Buckeyes	37
Caramel Applejack Balls	38
Caramel Brownies with Nuts	39,40
Caramel Corn	41
Carmel Pecan Cookies	42
Chess Bars	43,44
Chocolate Chip Cookies	45
Chocolate Cookie Candy	46
Chocolate Surprise Cookies	47
Christmas Wreath Cookies	48
Cornflake Cookies	49
Cornflake Flowers	50
Cow Pies	51
Crockpot Candy	52
Easy Pecan Sticky Buns	53
Forgotten Cookies	54
French Butter Cookies	55
Granny Moore's Christmas Cookies	56
Healthier No Bake Cookies	57
Homemade Peanut Butter Cups	58,59
Lace Cookies	60
Magic Cookie Bars	61
Martha Washington Candy	62
Mixed Nuts Millionaire Candy	63
No Cook Peanut Fudge	64
Oatmeal Raisin Cookies	65
Old Fashioned Potato Candy	66
Orange No-Bake Cookies	67
Oreo Truffles	68
Peanut Butter Cookies	69
Peanut Butter Cookies	69
Peanut Butter Crème Cookie Cups	70
Peanut Butter Surprises	71
Peppermint Bark	72
Pumpkin Fudge	73
Reindeer Cookies	74

Roberta Whoopie Pies	75
Rocky Road Squares	76
Rum Balls	76
Scaly Bark	77
Scotch Bars	78
Scrumptious Rice Krispies	79
S'mores Treats	80
Snickerdoodles	81
Strawberries	82
Unbaked Caramel Cookies	83
White Chocolate Peanut Butter Cookies	84

Cakes, Pies, and Miscellaneous — *Page*

Aunt Gwen's Pound Cake	85
Baptist Pound Cake	86
Banana Split Cake	87,88
Baskin Robbins Pie	89
Buttermilk Pie	90
Cherry Streusel Cheesecake	91
Chess Cake	92
Chocolate Chip Pound Cake	93
Chocolate Delight	94
Chocolate Pie	95
Chocolate Pecan Coconut Pie	96
Cinnamon Bun Pie	97
Citrus Pucker-Up Cake	98,99
Cream Cheese Pound Cake	100
Creamy Banana Pudding	101
Crustless Coconut Pie	102
Crustless Pumpkin Pie	103
Dried Apple Cake	104
Easy Ice Cream Cake	105
Easy White Chocolate Cheesecake	106
Fat-Free Banana Split Cake	107,108
Flan	109,110
Fluffy Ice Cream Frosty	111
Glazed Cherry Cream Cheese Danish	112,113
Granny's Cobbler	113
Granny Brown's Monkey Bread	114
Heavenly Orange Cheesecake	115,116
Ice Cream Pie	117
Impossible Pie	118
Jell-O Pies	119
Joy Cake	120,121

HOW TO SWAP BATCHES OF
COOKIES AND CANDY WITH OTHERS

Key Lime Cake	121,122
Lemonade Pie	123
Luscious Key Lime Cake	124,125
Mamow Edna's "Real Good" Cake	126
Mississippi Mud Cake	127,128
Momma's Coconut Cream Cake	128
Mountain Dew Apple Cake	129
Mrs. "Buck" Bracket Pound Cake	130
Orangesicle Cupcakes	131,132
Orange Juice Cake	133
Peach Cobbler	134
Peanut Butter Cake	135,136
Peanut Butter Pie	137
Peanut Butter Pie	138
Pecan Cobbler	139,140
Pina Colada Cake	141
Pineapple and Blueberry Cake	142
Plain Cheesecake	143
Popcorn Cake	144
Popcorn Cereal	144
Pumpkin Roll	145,146
Roberta's Cake	147
Simple Cheesecake	148
Snow Cake	149
Sour Cream Coconut Cake	150,151
Southern Sweet Citrus Pound Cake	152,153
Strawberry Daiquiri Cake	153
Strawberry Pecan Bread	154
Sugar-Free Double Dark Chocolate Cake	155,156

KATHERINE W. MASHBURN

REFERENCES FROM THE KITCHEN OF

LINDA ALLEN
Cookies and Candy
Old Fashioned Potato Candy
Peanut Butter Crème Cookie Cups
Cakes and Pies
Citrus Pucker-Up Cake
Heavenly Orange Cheesecake
Peanut Butter Cake
Sugar Free Double Dark Chocolate Cake

RENEE BAYNES
Cakes and Pies
Key Lime Cake
Pecan Cobbler

DIANE BEAN
Cakes and Pies
Pineapple and Blueberry Cake

BRENDA BLAYLOCK
Cookies and Candy
No Cook Peanut Fudge
Cakes and Pies
Chocolate Pecan Coconut Pie
Luscious Key Lime Cake
Miscellaneous
Fluffy Ice Cream Frosty

DONNA STONE BROWN
Cookies and Candy
Caramel Applejack Balls

NAN D. BROWN
Cakes and Pies
Granny Brown's Monkey Bread

HOW TO SWAP BATCHES OF COOKIES AND CANDY WITH OTHERS

YVONNE BURNS
Cookies and Candy
Homemade Peanut Butter Cups

BARBARA CALLAHAN
Cookies and Candy
Baker's One Bowl Chocolate Bliss Cookies
Chocolate Surprise Cookies
Cornflake Flowers
Oatmeal Raisin Cookies
Scrumptious Rice Krispies
Snickerdoodles
Unbaked Caramel Cookies
Cakes and Pies
Crustless Coconut Pie
Easy White Chocolate Cheesecake

NITA COCHRAN
Cakes and Pies
Momma's Coconut Cream Cake

MARY COKER
Cakes and Pies
Granny's Cobbler
Pina Colada Cake
Strawberry Daiquiri Cake

CHRISTY CRUMP
Cakes and Pies
Chess Cake

LISA DICKEY
Cookies and Candy
Black Bean Brownies (Gluten Free)
Healthier No-Bake Cookies
Peanut Butter Cookies
S'Mores Treats

KATHERINE W. MASHBURN

YVETTE DUNN
Cookies and Candy
Granny Moore's Christmas Cookies
Cakes and Pies
Mamow Edna's 'Real Good' Cake
Mrs. 'Buck' Bracket Pound Cake

BARBARA J. EARLY
Cookies and Candy
Peanut Butter Surprises
Roberta Whoopie Pies

KAREN ENGLAND
Cookies and Candy
Caramel Pecan Cookies
French Butter Cookies
Reindeer Cookies
Rocky Road Squares
Rum Balls

ELIZABETH FIELDEN
Cookies and Candy
A Favorite Candy
Chocolate Cookie Candy
Cornflake Cookies
Cow Pies
Crockpot Candy
Magic Cookie Bars
Mixed Nuts Millionaires Candy
Orange No-Bake Cookies
Peppermint Bark
Strawberries
White Chocolate Peanut Butter Cookies
Cakes and Pies
Baptist Pound Cake
Baskin Robbins Pie
Creamy Banana Pudding

HOW TO SWAP BATCHES OF COOKIES AND CANDY WITH OTHERS

Crustless Pecan Pie
Mountain Dew Apple Cake
Pumpkin Roll
Roberta's Cake
Snow Cake
Strawberry Pecan Bread

JENNIFER MASHBURN HAMBRIGHT
Cookies and Candy
Oreo Truffles

MISSY GIBSON HIGHTOWER
Cakes and Pies
Cherry Streusel Cheesecake

POLLY JONES
Cakes and Pies
Orange Juice Cake

BROOKE KEELER
Cakes & Pies
Chocolate Chip Pound Cake
Chocolate Delight
Chocolate Pie
Dried Apple Cake
Peach Cobbler

SHAUNA LEATHERWOOD
Cookies and Candy
Caramel Brownies with Nuts

DARLENE LUCAS
Cookies and Candy
Martha Washington Candy
Cakes and Pies
Impossible Pie
Jell-O Pies
Southern Sweet Citrus Pound Cake

KATHERINE W. MASHBURN

KATHY MASHBURN
Cookies and Candy
Blonde Brownies
Chocolate Chip Cookies
Easy Pecan Sticky Buns
Cakes and Pies
Cinnamon Bun Pie
Easy Ice Cream Cake
Glazed Cherry Cream Cheese Danish
Plain Cheesecake

CINDY MCENTYRE
Cookies and Candy
Caramel Corn
Chess Bars
Lace Cookies
Scaly Bark
Cakes and Pies
Flan
Joy Cake
Mississippi Mud Cake
Sour Cream Coconut Cake

RACHEL MOREHEAD
Cookies and Candy
Scotch Bars
Cakes and Pies
Lemonade Pie

SHERRY MOSS
Cookies and Candy
Forgotten Cookies
Cakes and Pies
Cream Cheese Pound Cake

BRANDI NAGY
Cakes and Pies
Peanut Butter Pie

HOW TO SWAP BATCHES OF COOKIES AND CANDY WITH OTHERS

CYNDI BEST OWENBY
Cookies and Candy
Christmas Wreath Cookies
Cakes and Pies
Banana Split Cake

KATHRYN OWENS
Cakes and Pies
Peanut Butter Pie

RACHEL OWENS
Cookies and Candy
Buckeyes
Cakes and Pies
Buttermilk Pie

SABRINA OWENS
Cookies and Candy
Pumpkin Fudge
Cakes and Pies
Orangesicle Cupcakes

CINDY OWNBY
Cakes and Pies
Popcorn Cake

GWEN BROWN PRITCHETT
Cakes and Pies
Aunt Gwen's Pound Cake

ESPERANZA REYES
Miscellaneous
Popcorn Cereal

NATALIE SMITH
Cookies and Candy
Peanut Butter Cookies

KATHERINE W. MASHBURN

Cakes and Pies
Aunt Gwen's Pound Cake
Granny Brown's Monkey Bread
Ice Cream Pie
Momma's Coconut Cream Cake

LISA VICKERY
Cakes and Pies
Fat-Free Banana Split Cake

MELINDA WILLIAMS
Cakes and Pies
Simple Cheesecake

The following brands are registered trademarks ® including Applejack, Kraft, Honey Graham, Pet, Ritz, Crisco, M&M's Stevia, Rolos, Hershey, Baker's, Eagle Brand, Reeses, Oreo, Pam, Betty Crocker, Duncan Hines, Jell-O, Tropical Isle, Rice Krispies, Pringles, Pillsbury, Baskin Robbins, Mountain Dew, Splenda, and Planters. Certain brands are suggested in some recipes.

www.ingramcontent.com/pod-product-compliance
Lightning Source LLC
Chambersburg PA
CBHW061325040426
42444CB00011B/2779